MODERN DAY PRESIDENTIAL

@realDonaldTrump

PREMIER CLASSICS

Published by the East India Publishing Company
9781989201503

© 2018 East India Publishing Company

All rights reserved. No part of this book may be reproduced by any manner without the express written consent of the publisher, except in cases of brief excerpts in critical reviews and articles.

Cover Design by EIPC. © 2018

PRINTED IN THE UNITED STATES OF AMERICA

CONTENTS

An Inconvenient Lie	7
Only Rosie O'Donnell	15
Kenyan Born Muslim Interloper	23
Taming the RINO	30
Crooked Hillary	70
Build that Wall	95
Radical Islamic Terrorism	122
Enemy of the People	127
Rocket Man	161
Obstructionist Losers	177

An Inconvenient Lie

It snowed over 4 inches this past weekend in New York City. It is still October. So much for Global Warming. 1 Nov 2011 19:43

Newly released emails prove that scientists have manipulated data on global warming. The data is unreliable. 30 Nov 2011 18:25

Global warming has been proven to be a canard repeatedly over and over again. The left needs a dose of reality. 28 Mar 2012 18:43

Waste! With a $16T debt and $1T budget deficit @BarackObama is sending $770M overseas "to fight global warming" 30 Mar 2012 17:55

According to @BarackObama the War on Terror is over but global warming is a national (cont) 4 May 2012 20:12

In the 1920's people were worried about global cooling--it never happened. Now it's global warming. Give me a break! 4 May 2012 20:13

Do you believe @algore is blaming global warming for the hurricane? 1 Nov 2012 14:13

Let's continue to destroy the competitiveness of our factories & manufacturing so we can fight mythical global warming. China is so happy! 1 Nov 2012 14:23

Global warming is based on faulty science and manipulated data which is proven by the emails that were leaked 2 Nov 2012 18:59

It's extremely cold in NY & NJ—not good for flood victims. Where is global warming? 5 Nov 2012 15:55

Great article in the @NewYorkPost by Ben Garrett--"Don't Blame Sandy on Global Warming" 5 Nov 2012 16:06

We can't destroy the competitiveness of our factories in order to prepare for nonexistent global warming. China is thrilled with us! 5 Nov 2012 16:50

The concept of global warming was created by and for the Chinese in order to make U.S. manufacturing non-competitive. 6 Nov 2012 19:15

It's freezing and snowing in New York--we need global warming! 7 Nov 2012 19:24

It is snowing in Jerusalem and across Lebanon. Global warming! 14 Jan 2013 21:10

Watch Obama push major global warming legislation early in his second term... 24 Jan 2013 20:13

The freezing cold weather across the country is brutal. Must be all that global warming. 25 Jan 2013 19:50

It's snowing & freezing in NYC. What the hell ever happened to global warming? 21 Mar 2013 14:25

Looks like the U.S. will be having the coldest March since 1996-global warming anyone????????? 22 Mar 2013 20:07

It's springtime and it just started snowing in NYC. What is going on with global warming? 25 Mar 2013 18:14

They changed the name from "global warming" to "climate change" after the term global warming just wasn't working (it was too cold)! 25 Mar 2013 18:15

UK is freezing through longest & coldest winter in over 50 years Where's the global warming? @gatewaypundit 25 Mar 2013 18:19

Another freezing day in the Spring - what is going on with "global warming"? Good move changing the name to "climate change" - sad! 3 Apr 2013 9:14

It's freezing in New York—where the hell is global warming? 23 Apr 2013 19:37

Wrong used to be called global warming and when that name didn't work they deftly changed it to climate change-because it's freezing! 24 Apr 2013 1:45

Snow and freezing weather all over mid-section of Country. Global warming specialists better start thinking fast! 1 May 2013 13:04

32º in New York - it's freezing! Where the hell is global warming when you need it? 14 May 2013 10:30

It's freezing outside where the hell is "global warming"?? 25 May 2013 23:00

It's 46º (really cold) and snowing in New York on Memorial Day - tell the so-called "scientists" that we want global warming right now! 27 May 2013 11:21

We are being embarrassed by Russia and China on Snowden (and much more) yet Obama is talking about global warming on Tuesday. 24 Jun 2013 18:26

For the disciples of global warming in 150 summers (years) there have been 20 heat waves as bad or worse than current-this has happened b4! 18 Jul 2013 23:15

Surprise? 1970's global cooling alarmists were pushing same no-growth liberal agenda as today's global warming 31 Jul 2013 19:44

So much for 'global warming.' Earth is cooling at a record pace 9 Sep 2013 21:44

Where's the global warming? 2013 was one of the least extreme years in weather on record 21 Oct 2013 18:26

I wonder if the Rutgers coach who had the audacity to yell at the player is a proponent of global warming? 17 Nov 2013 23:31

Snow and ice freezing weather in Texas Arizona and Oklahoma - what the hell is going on with GLOBAL WARMING? 23 Nov 2013 13:09

The people that gave you global warming are the same people that gave you ObamaCare! 24 Nov 2013 1:16

They changed the name global warming to climate change because the concept of global warming just wasn't working! 24 Nov 2013 1:23

The least number of hurricanes in the U.S. in decades. So they change global warming (too cold) to climate change-now what will they call it 2 Dec 2013 13:46

Denver Minnesota and others are bracing for some of the coldest weather on record. What are the global warming geniuses saying about this? 3 Dec 2013 23:42

Wow record setting cold temperatures throughout large parts of the country. Must be global warming I mean climate change! 4 Dec 2013 23:40

The problem w/ the concept of "global warming" is that the U.S. is spending a fortune on "fixing it" while China & others do nothing! 5 Dec 2013 13:54

Ice storm rolls from Texas to Tennessee - I'm in Los Angeles and it's freezing. Global warming is a total and very expensive hoax! 6 Dec 2013 15:13

We should be focused on magnificently clean and healthy air and not distracted by the expensive hoax that is global warming! 6 Dec 2013 15:38

This is one of the COLDEST WINTERS ever freezing all over the country for long periods of time! So much for GLOBAL WARMING. 12 Dec 2013 11:38

Wow it's snowing in Isreal and on the pyramids in Egypt. Are we still wasting billions on the global warming con? MAKE U.S. COMPETITIVE! 15 Dec 2013 0:32

59% of the United States by area is now covered in snow-highest % in many years. The "global warming" name isn't working anymore-SORRY! 15 Dec 2013 9:38

They call it "climate change" now because the words "global warming" didn't work anymore. Same people fighting hard to keep it all going! 15 Dec 2013 9:58

We should be focusing on beautiful clean air & not on wasteful & very expensive GLOBAL WARMING bullshit! China & others are hurting our air 15 Dec 2013 10:07

It is really too bad that the scientists studying GLOBAL WARMING in Antarctica got stuck on their icebreaker because of massive ice and cold 27 Dec 2013 12:02

The rescue icebreaker trying to free the ship of the GLOBAL WARMING scientists has turned back-the ice is massive (a record). IRONIC! 28 Dec 2013 12:20

We should be focused on clean and beautiful air-not expensive and business closing GLOBAL WARMING-a total hoax! 28 Dec 2013 12:30

An Inconvenient Lie

The global warming scientists don't want to be the ship-they are having too much fun and that is a solution-FAME! 28 Dec 2013 12:37

Temperature at record lows in many parts of the country. 50 degrees below zero with wind chill in large area. Global warming folks iced in! 29 Dec 2013 23:08

What the hell is going on with GLOBAL WARMING. The planet is freezing the ice is building and the G.W. scientists are stuck-a total con job 31 Dec 2013 0:34

The con artists changed the name from GLOBAL WARMING to CLIMATE CHANGE when GLOBAL WARMING was no longer working and credibility was lost! 31 Dec 2013 0:44

This very expensive GLOBAL WARMING bullshit has got to stop. Our planet is freezing record low tempsand our GW scientists are stuck in ice 2 Jan 2014 0:39

Record snowfall & freezing temps throughout the country. Where is Global Warming when you need it?! 3 Jan 2014 20:29

We are experiencing the coldest weather in more than two decades-most people never remember anything like this. GLOBAL WARMING anyone? 6 Jan 2014 23:19

NBC News just called it the great freeze - coldest weather in years. Is our country still spending money on the GLOBAL WARMING HOAX? 25 Jan 2014 23:48

Any and all weather events are used by the GLOBAL WARMING HOAXSTERS to justify higher taxes to save our planet! They don't believe it $$$$! 26 Jan 2014 21:40

Snowing in Texas and Louisiana record setting freezing temperatures throughout the country and beyond. Global warming is an expensive hoax! 29 Jan 2014 6:27

The weather has been so cold for so long that the global warming HOAXSTERS were forced to change the name to climate change to keep $ flow! 29 Jan 2014 6:36

Give me clean beautiful and healthy air - not the same old climate change (global warming) bullshit! I am tired of hearing this nonsense. 29 Jan 2014 6:44

With one of the worst and most prolonged cold spells in his-

@realDonaldTrump

tory with Atlanta Texas and parts of Florida freezing- Global Warming anyone? 30 Jan 2014 2:46

Obama said in his SOTU that "global warming is a fact." Sure about as factual as "if you like your healthcare you can keep it." 30 Jan 2014 18:14

Watch commodity prices soar because of the freezing cold. Will be bad for the economy. We could use some global warming. 3 Feb 2014 19:48

Massive record setting snowstorm and freezing temperatures in U.S. Smart that GLOBAL WARMING hoaxsters changed name to CLIMATE CHANGE! $$$$ 5 Feb 2014 10:57

When will our country stop wasting money on global warming and so many other truly "STUPID" things and begin to focus on lower taxes? 5 Feb 2014 11:01

A big part of the country even the southern states is under massive attack from snow and freezing cold. Global warming anyone? 13 Feb 2014 18:46

Don't let the GLOBAL WARMING wiseguys get away with changing the name to CLIMATE CHANGE because the FACTS do not let GW tag to work anymore! 17 Feb 2014 12:39

It's not climate changeit's global warming.Don't let the dollar sucking wiseguys change names midstream because the first name didn't work 18 Feb 2014 0:38

Congrats to Charles @krauthammer for his statements on climate change formerly known as global warming! 26 Feb 2014 21:22

Baltimore just set a record for the coldest day in March in a long recorded history - 4 degrees. Other places likewise. Global warming con! 4 Mar 2014 11:29

In New York March was the coldest month in recorded history - we could use some GLOBAL WARMING! 1 Apr 2014 12:06

The global warming we should be worried about is the global warming caused by NUCLEAR WEAPONS in the hands of crazy or incompetent leaders! 8 May 2014 3:53

I wonder if when Secy. Kerry goes to Iraq and Afghanistan he pushes hard for them to look at GLOBAL WARMING and study the carbon footprint? 23 Jun 2014 16:26

Record cold temperatures in July - 20 to 30 degrees colder than normal. What the hell happened to GLOBAL WARMING? 14 Jul 2014 22:33

They only changed the term to CLIMATE CHANGE when the words GLOBAL WARMING didn't work anymore. Come on people get smart! 14 Jul 2014 23:19

The only global warming that people should be concerned with is the global warming caused by nuclear weapons because of our weak U.S. leader 15 Jul 2014 0:22

Tremendous cold wave hits large part of U.S. Lucky they changed the name from global warming to climate change - G.W. just doesn't work! 16 Jul 2014 12:11

It's late in July and it is really cold outside in New York. Where the hell is GLOBAL WARMING??? We need some fast! It's now CLIMATE CHANGE 29 Jul 2014 1:47

Windmills are the greatest threat in the US to both bald and golden eagles. Media claims fictional 'global warming' is worse. 9 Sep 2014 20:19

Great article on so-called climate change formerly known as global warming. 17 Sep 2014 14:26

As ISIS and Ebola spread like wildfire the Obama administration just submitted a paper on how to stop climate change (aka global warming). 14 Oct 2014 3:17

Just out - the POLAR ICE CAPS are at an all time high the POLAR BEAR population has never been stronger. Where the hell is global warming? 29 Oct 2014 9:15

The entire country is FREEZING - we desperately need a heavy dose of global warming and fast! Ice caps size reaches all time high. 17 Nov 2014 4:24

Just like Jonathan Gruber viciously lied & called Americans "stupid" on ObamaCare many consultants are doing the same on Global Warming. 18 Nov 2014 15:30

There are many Jonathan Gruber types selling the global warming "stuff" - and they really do believe the American public is stupid. 19 Nov 2014 0:59

For those that constantly say that "global warming" is now "climate change"—they changed the name. The name global warming wasn't working 19 Nov 2014 16:10

It's record cold all over the country and world - where the hell is global warming we need some fast! 8 Jan 2015 10:21

Where the hell is global warming when you need it? 26 Jan 2015 23:18

Record low temperatures and massive amounts of snow. Where the hell is GLOBAL WARMING? 15 Feb 2015 4:23

Wow 25 degrees below zero record cold and snow spell. Global warming anyone? 15 Feb 2015 23:37

Among the lowest temperatures EVER in much of the United States. Ice caps at record size. Changed name from GLOBAL WARMING to CLIMATE CHANGE 18 Feb 2015 12:17

Record setting cold and snow ice caps massive! The only global warming we should fear is that caused by nuclear weapons - incompetent pols. 19 Feb 2015 12:33

It's really cold outside they are calling it a major freeze weeks ahead of normal. Man we could use a big fat dose of global warming! 19 Oct 2015 13:30

In the East it could be the COLDEST New Year's Eve on record. Perhaps we could use a little bit of that good old Global Warming that our Country but not other countries was going to pay TRILLIONS OF DOLLARS to protect against. Bundle up! 29 Dec 2017 0:01

Brutal and Extended Cold Blast could shatter ALL RECORDS - Whatever happened to Global Warming? 22 Nov 2018 0:23

Only Rosie O'Donnell (and other celebrity fueds)

@macmiller "Donald Trump the Song" gets 16M hits on YouTube. Who wouldn't be flattered? 12 Jul 2011 20:08

@MacMiller will enjoy today's #trumpvlog... 18 Aug 2011 14:28

#trumpvlog Same last name same bad ratings- @lawrence and @rosie..... 14 Dec 2011 15:11

I feel sorry for Rosie 's new partner in love whose parents are devastated at the thought of their daughter being with @Rosie--a true loser. 14 Dec 2011 16:45

#badratings @Rosie you will never make it. You are not funny or talented. 14 Dec 2011 17:19

Save your time @rosie and focus on your horrible ratings and don't mention my name on talk shows anymore or you will get more of the same. 14 Dec 2011 17:20

With the number of tweets sad sack @Rosie has done she has totally lost control of herself-- hopefully not a breakdown. 15 Dec 2011 15:56

Please send a psychiatrist to help @Rosie she's in a bad state. To @Rosie's girlfriend's parents--- get (cont) 15 Dec 2011 17:05

Rosie O'Donnell's show is "dead"- can't keep going for long with such poor ratings. @Rosie is a stone cold (cont) 17 Jan 2012 15:29

@fatmaninaspeedo I have not met @MacMiller but his song Donald Trump has had over 40 milion hits. Maybe he should pay me somethiing. 8 Feb 2012 20:01

My @foxandfriends interview where I discuss @Rosie being canceled yet again and how she just can't make it on TV 19 Mar 2012 16:26

I am so glad @Rosie got fired by @Oprah. Rosie is a bully and it's always nice to see bullies go down! 20 Mar 2012 14:54

He @RickSantorum has as much chance of being the GOP nominee as @Rosie does of ever having a successful (cont) 21 Mar 2012 15:30

#trumpvlog The song "Donald Trump" hits 54 million views. @MacMiller- Where's my money? 20 Apr 2012 15:05

Rosie O'Donnell should leave Lindsay Lohan alone--@Rosie has bigger problems than Lindsay. Lindsay's mother called my office for help 30 Apr 2012 16:01

Good Morning America is thrilled @Rosie is working for the @todayshow--that means almost guaranteed success for @GMA 30 Apr 2012 16:57

.@Cher attacked @MittRomney. She is an average talent who is out of touch with reality. Like @Rosie O'Donnell a total loser! 10 May 2012 15:10

My @gretawire interview discussing @BarackObama's misleading political ad @MittRomney's response and @Cher & @Rosie 15 May 2012 18:45

Rapper @MacMiller's song "Donald Trump" now has 57 million hits--- I created another star--- where's my cut? 22 May 2012 15:14

Losers such as George Will and @Rosie use me to get publicity for themselves. They are strictly third rate. 29 May 2012 15:48

.@MacMiller's "Donald Trump" just hit 60 million hits. Maybe I should go into a new business. 20 Jun 2012 19:14

.@MacMiller's 'Donald Trump' song is at 64.5M views on YouTube You're welcome Mac! 9 Aug 2012 19:01

.@Rosie get better fast. I'm starting to miss you! 21 Aug 2012 16:36

Hey @Rosie--how is your recovery going? I hope you are doing well so we can start fighting again soon! 18 Oct 2012 21:06

@Rosie @realDonaldTrump Thanks for the info Rosie--get well. 19 Oct 2012 14:25

.@Toure when you are fired from MSNBC for your bad ratings and racist coverage stop by and say hello. 22 Oct 2012 16:29

.@Toure I felt very sorry for you during your meltdown on @PiersMorgan. He drove you insane but of course Piers is a lot smarter than you 22 Oct 2012 19:28

.@BarbaraJWalters @theviewtv will apologize to me just like she did when I was right about @Rosie. Besides I get great ratings on The View. 25 Oct 2012 16:46

She's baaack! @Rosie needs me to salvage her dying career. But it won't help-- she's got no talent & no persona. Too many tv cancellations! 9 Nov 2012 21:02

I am going to give @Rosie a pass. @Rosie is desperate to get back on TV so she can be on yet another show that can be quickly canceled. 20 Nov 2012 19:29

I was nice to loser @rosie and she attacked me--it just shows never let up with a bully. They only fade when you hit them hard! 20 Nov 2012 19:29

.@Lord_Sugar If you think ugly windmills are good for Scotland you are an even worse businessman than I thought... 6 Dec 2012 20:56

Sugar: @Lord_Sugar—unlike you I own The Apprentice. You were never successful enough... 6 Dec 2012 21:07

Sugar: @Lord_Sugar--Keep working hard so I make plenty of $ with your show... 6 Dec 2012 21:22

@piersmorgan @Lord_Sugar I easily could but as long as Sugar is making me money (it's my show) I won't--unlike Sugar I'm not stupid! 6 Dec 2012 21:59

Dopey @Lord_Sugar—Look in the mirror and thank the real Lord that Donald Trump exists. You are nothing! 6 Dec 2012 22:08

@Lord_Sugar @piersmorgan Sugar if you taught Piers Morgan he never would have won! 6 Dec 2012 22:33

Sugar @Lord_Sugar—you should say thank you Donald like a good little boy... ... 6 Dec 2012 22:42

@piersmorgan @Lord_Sugar No his ignorance! 6 Dec 2012 22:50

Sugar @Lord_Sugar Unlike yours my financials are phenomenal. People don't know your real numbers & would not be impressed. 7 Dec 2012 15:34

Sugar @Lord_Sugar Why don't you tell the public what you're really worth--they would be very disappointed. 7 Dec 2012 15:35

Dopey Sugar @Lord_Sugar--I'm worth more than $8 billion acknowledged almost no debt ... 7 Dec 2012 16:31

Dopey Sugar.@Lord_Sugar ...Your net worth doesn't even qualify you to host the Apprentice. Keep making me money. 7 Dec 2012 16:36

.@Lord_Sugar - nice call on predicting that the iPOD would be "dead finished gone kaput" Great business foresight. 7 Dec 2012 16:37

.@Lord_Sugar....but you wouldn't notice because you have no vision and you are a total loser. 7 Dec 2012 17:02

Dopey Sugar @Lord_Sugar The wind turbines are ruining the beauty & majesty of Scotland... 7 Dec 2012 17:02

...@Lord_Sugar You need the income from the show to keep going--hope it doesn't hurt. 7 Dec 2012 17:46

Dopey @Lord_Sugar People are calling in saying you are being beaten badly w/ the tweets... 7 Dec 2012 17:46

Dopey @Lord_Sugar I'm worth $8 billion and you're worth peanuts...without my show nobody would even know who you are. 7 Dec 2012 17:48

Dopey Sugar @Lord_Sugar I never go silent. I was buying a major property in Florida--a property worth more than you are! 10 Dec 2012 15:14

Dopey Sugar @Lord_Sugar I hear your ratings last week were at an all time low--you better get them up or you'll be fired. 10 Dec 2012 15:15

Dopey Sugar @Lord_Sugar Bad ratings--come on keep making me money--remember I own your show. 10 Dec 2012 15:16

Dopey Sugar—@Lord_Sugar Isn't it sad that my golf course in Scotland just got "best new course in the world"—it's worth more than you are! 10 Dec 2012 16:14

Dopey Sugar @Lord_Sugar You should thank me for having created the platform on which you became known--The Apprentice. Say Thank you Donald 10 Dec 2012 17:24

.@Lord_Sugar If you didn't say the iPod would be gone in a year you might have been really rich instead of the peanut money you have. 10 Dec 2012 17:56

Dopey Sugar @Lord_Sugar—you are the worst kind of loser—a total fool. 10 Dec 2012 18:05

@Nc777ww He is a loser who will self-destruct just like @Rosie! 21 Dec 2012 14:46

.@Rosie--If America's Got Talent uses you the show will fail like all your others! 21 Dec 2012 16:17

Dopey @Rosie--I never went bankrupt--ABC already apologized to me for your stupid statement in the past--they didn't want a lawsuit. 21 Dec 2012 16:20

@Skyhawk442 @Rosie I agree! 23 Dec 2012 15:03

.@MacMiller's "Donald Trump" just crossed 73.5 million views on @YouTube. You're welcome Mac! 27 Dec 2012 20:51

@HShoyeb @Lord_Sugar @piersmorgan Thanks 7 Jan 2013 19:53

My @extratv interview discussing @Rosie's new baby my acceptance of @billmaher's $5M offer & hiring @_KatherineWebb 10 Jan 2013 19:08

Little @MacMiller sent me an expensive plaque for making his song "Donald Trump" such a big hit. Mac you still... 31 Jan 2013 18:03

Little @MacMiller—I don't need your praise - just pay me the money you owe. 31 Jan 2013 18:09

@TiffanyBrownInc @MacMiller Not really! 31 Jan 2013 19:43

Little @MacMiller you illegally used my name for your song "Donald Trump" which now has over 75 million hits. 31 Jan 2013 20:45

Little @MacMiller I want the money not the plaque you gave me! 31 Jan 2013 20:50

Little @MacMiller I'm now going to teach you a big boy lesson about lawsuits and finance. You ungrateful dog! 31 Jan 2013 21:03

See ungrateful Little @MacMiller's statement to me a year ago— he was kissing my ass! 31 Jan 2013 21:45

Little @MacMiller—I have more hair than you do and there's a slight age difference. 31 Jan 2013 21:46

@droppinloads29 @billmaher @Rosie But Rosie is smarter than @billmaher 13 Feb 2013 19:10

It was just announced that @MacMiller's song "DonaldTrump" went platinum—tell Mac Miller to kiss my ass! 6 Mar 2013 16:54

.@MacMiller has over 79M hits on YouTube & just hit platinum with his Donald Trump song—screw you Mac! 22 Apr 2013 16:13

The big problem for little @MacMiller is that he's going to have to have another hit song not just his Donald Trump bonanza. 22 Apr 2013 16:13

@Lord_Sugar can't hold a.candle to Donald.Trump - he is a laughing stock in Great Britain (but his show pays me lots of money so I'm happy) 11 May 2013 21:25

@Lord_Sugar Much more than anybody knows dopey much more - and it will soon be revealed in detail. 19 May 2013 13:21

Not only is @Toure a racist (and boring) he's a really dumb guy! 13 Aug 2013 2:36

#TrumpVine Where is the money @MacMiller? 15 Aug 2013 14:38

@DanScavino @MacMiller Thanks Dan. 15 Aug 2013 15:45

@KeithJMcConnell @MacMiller Thanks. 15 Aug 2013 18:39

The ratings of The Cycle on MSNBC a sad and pathetic show are way down. If they fired racist moron @Toure a truly stupid guy they live! 30 Aug 2013 19:10

@Toure If you weren't such a dumb racist moron with bad ratings you would know I never filed for bankruptcynow worth over $10 billion dummy 10 Sep 2013 1:44

@Toure Dumb as a rock Toure doesn't have a clue about money or anything else-merely a simpleton racist.Really bad ratingsreally stupid guy 10 Sep 2013 1:53

@Toure Why does a network allow a stupid racist like Toure to stay on the air when his ratings are so abysmal! Can there be only one reason 10 Sep 2013 2:10

@CARepublican12 @Toure So true! 10 Sep 2013 20:28

.@Rosie—No offense and good luck on the new show but remember you started it! 25 Sep 2014 20:03

Just as I predicted @Rosie would fail on The View 1 Dec 2014 15:42

Ratings way down show irrelevant. Why haven't they learned? @Rosie always fails. 1 Dec 2014 15:44

Rosie O'Donnell went after me again on The View in order to stir up her failing ratings. Nothing will help her--@Rosie always fails. 1 Dec 2014 16:08

#TrumpVlog @Rosie needs to rest and relax. It's not working. 1 Dec 2014 16:31

#TrumpVlog @Rosie wasn't even a short term fix at The View. 1 Dec 2014 20:25

.@WhoopiGoldberg Don't let @Rosie speak badly of you or try to bring you down. She is rude crude & not smart. She is not in your league. 1 Dec 2014 20:59

No surprise. @Rosie is failing on @TheView.Terrible ratings."Malcontent" & another season is "out of the question" 1 Dec 2014 22:02

It's Tuesday. How many more 'The View' Execs will leak that they want @rosie gone? Show is failing. 2 Dec 2014 21:36

Sorry @Rosie is a mentally sick woman a bully a dummy and above all a loser. Other than that she is just wonderful! 9 Dec 2014 1:53

.@Lord_Sugar How did you enjoy Mar-a-Lago? It was nice having you there--my people thought you were terrific! 27 Jan 2015 16:51

Made in America? @BarackObama called his 'birthplace' Hawaii "here in Asia." 18 Nov 2011 10:54

Kenyan Born Muslim Interloper

When I was 18, people called me Donald Trump. When he was 18, @BarackObama was Barry Soweto. Weird. 12 Mar 2012 10:34

He @BarackObama wants 23 years of @MittRomney's tax returns. Let's see BHO's school applications, transcripts and Rezkko deals. I wonder what they say about his place of birth--how were his grades (I think I know). Demand their release. 10 Apr 2012 14:29

I wonder if @BarackObama ever applied to Occidental, Columbia or Harvard as a foreign student. When can we see his applications? What do they say about his place of birth. 22 May 2012 15:34

.@BarackObama is practically begging @MittRomney to disavow the place of birth movement, he is afraid of it and for good reason. He keeps using @SenJohnMcCain as an example, however, @SenJohnMcCain lost the election. Don't let it happen again. 29 May 2012 10:37

I want to see @BarackObama's college records to see how he listed his place of birth in the application. 30 May 2012 11:44

In his own words, @BarackObama "was born in Kenya, and raised in Indonesia and Hawaii." This statement was made, in writing, in the 1990's. Why does the press protect him? Is this another Watergate? 30 May 2012 13:13

.@MittRomney should not give any other further information until @BarackObama releases the things that everyone wants to see---- 10 Jul 2012 8:35

.@BarackObama wants to see 10 yrs of @MittRomney's tax returns--tell him "ok--but we want to see your college applications first.' 13 Jul 2012 13:03

My @foxandfriends interview discussing how @BarackObama should release his college applications & records 16 Jul 2012 14:53

If @BarackObama had such a wonderful academic record why wouldn't he want to show it? 17 Jul 2012 11:38

.@BarackObama's college application would be very very very very interesting! 17 Jul 2012 11:54

When will we see @BarackObama's passport records (sealed)? 17 Jul 2012 15:18

For the sake of transparency, @BarackObama should release all his college applications and transcripts--both from Occidental and Columbia. 17 Jul 2012 15:53

I hope @MittRomney now starts asking for any & all of @BarackObama's sealed records--it's time. 17 Jul 2012 12:10

Why would @BarackObama be spending millions of dollars to hide his records if there was nothing to hide? 17 Jul 2012 15:30

Weird--why did BarackObama Sr. fail to list @BarackObama as his son in his 1961 INS application? 18 Jul 2012 9:26

Congratulations to @RealSheriffJoe on his successful Cold Case Posse investigation which claims @BarackObama's 'birth certificate' is fake 18 Jul 2012 10:56

As I always said, the "Birthers" were after the truth. Thanks to @RealSheriffJoe @BarackObama can't hide anymore. 18 Jul 2012 12:45

What's more important for the American public to have? @MittRomney's tax returns or @BarackObama's sealed records? 18 Jul 2012 13:16

I am impressed with the scam @BarackObama pulled, but the truth will come out. 20 Jul 2012 8:29

With @BarackObama listing himself as "Born in Kenya" in 1999 HI laws allowed him to produce a fake certificate. #SCAM 20 Jul 2012 9:07

Jay Carney won't answer reporters questions of "Why Obama won't release his college transcripts"- Come on, Jay! 23 Jul 2012 15:21

In '08, @BarackObama hit Bush for secrecy When will Obama release all his sealed college records?! 2 Aug 2012 13:53

An 'extremely credible source' has called my office & told me that @BarackObama applied to Occidental as a foreign student--think about it! 6 Aug 2012 15:20

An 'extremely credible source' has called my office and told me that @BarackObama's birth certificate is a fraud. 6 Aug 2012 15:23

I wonder if @BarackObama ever had an Indonesian passport. Did he become an Indonesian citizen when he lived there? 9 Aug 2012 11:35

RT @IBDeditorials: Was Barack Obama A Foreign Exchange Student? 10 Aug 2012 14:06

.@MittRomney shouldn't give additional tax returns until @BarackObama gives his passport records, college records & applications... 17 Aug 2012 8:14

Many people will be surprised at what is about to be released concerning @BarackObama's background. I, for one, won't be. 22 Aug 2012 8:48

Why do the Republicans keep apologizing on the so called "birther" issue? No more apologies--take the offensive! 27 Aug 2012 10:58

Media silent when @BarackObama called @MittRomney a murderer & felon. Mitt mentions 'birth certificate' and they go nuts. Double standard! 28 Aug 2012 8:37

What a coincidence--Michelle Obama called Kenya @BarackObama's "homeland" in 2008 29 Aug 2012 9:02

The media can track down @PaulRyan's old girlfriend and marathon time but can't find @BarackObama's college applications or other info. 4 Sep 2012 14:51

Why won't Obama release his college applications? Is there something 'foreign' about them? 11 Sep 2012 14:08

Why has Barack Obama repeatedly told inconsistent stories about his religious background? Who is he? 11 Sep 2012 8:42

Wake Up America! See article: "Israeli Science: Obama Birth Certificate is a Fake" 13 Sep 2012 10:40

.@MittRomney must ask for Obama's college records & applications--why is he not doing this? 27 Sep 2012 15:05

In debate, @MittRomney should ask Obama why autobiography states "born in Kenya, raised in Indonesia." 1 Oct 2012 14:21

If Obama mentions Mitt's tax returns in tomorrow's debate then Mitt should immediately ask for Obama's college records & applications 2 Oct 2012 10:49

The public is about to learn a lot more information on Barack Obama and his true background in the coming weeks... 9 Oct 2012 22:06

So Obama used to tell classmates that he was Kenyan royalty and an Indonesian prince. Sounds like his book bio! 11 Oct 2012 14:59

Isn't it time that Obama release his college records and applications? Boy would that create a mess! He is not who you think. 15 Oct 2012 11:55

Do you believe Barack Hussein Obama (aka Barry Soetoro) looked like a president last night? I don't! 17 Oct 2012 9:16

If Obama goes after Mitt's private sector experience in the next debate then Mitt should ask for Obama's college records--all of them. 17 Oct 2012 15:09

RT @APCampaign:Trump to Obama: $5 million donation to charity if you release passport and college records #Election2012 24 Oct 2012 16:41

I am happy to donate $5 million to a charity Barack Obama chooses. All I am asking is that he is transparent with the American people 24 Oct 2012 16:43

Obama has no problem leaking national security secrets. Why can't he release his records? Especially when $5M is going to charity. 24 Oct 2012 16:44

My offer to Obama is about transparency. In 2008, American people were sold on hope and change. This our last chance to get the full record. 24 Oct 2012 16:26

RT @ReutersPolitics: Trump to give $5 million to charity if Obama releases records 24 Oct 2012 16:22

... By releasing his records, he can come clean with the American people and have $5 million go to a charity. 24 Oct 2012 16:49

For someone who demanded 20 years of Mitt's tax returns, you would think my offer to donate $5M to charity for his records is an easy go. 25 Oct 2012 15:15

It is really a shame that Barack Obama may stop $5M from being generously donated to charity all because he refuses to be transparent. 25 Oct 2012 16:06

I am offering the chance for Barack Obama to redistribute $5M to any charity of his choice. Everyone wins. Take the deal. 25 Oct 2012 12:01

"Trump Offers To Donate $5 Million To Charity If Obama Releases College Transcripts" via @rcpvideo 25 Oct 2012 13:15

The Letterman show really turned things around- people finally understand my $5 million dollar offer to charity.... 26 Oct 2012 9:52

Barack Obama has everything to gain. Why would anyone ever deny $5M to charity? 26 Oct 2012 15:21

If my offer is refused, every undecided OH voter will be fully aware that Obama denied $5M to charity all because he is hiding something! 26 Oct 2012 15:23

If Obama doesn't accept my offer to be fully transparent, what will he say? 26 Oct 2012 15:26

Watch Obama's favorability numbers drop even further if he doesn't accept my charitable offer. No one approves (cont) 26 Oct 2012 15:28

Another great charity that the $5M could go to just a recommendation to the Pres. - the Wounded Warriors represented so well by @TraceAdkins 26 Oct 2012 9:02

I have decided to add a caveat to my offer. Obama can't decide to send my $5M to Rev. Wright if he releases his records. 26 Oct 2012 14:55

Another great cause Obama could send my $5M donation to is a charity for 9/11 First Responders. They are American heroes. 30 Oct 2012 12:32

Why does Obama believe he shouldn't comply with record releases that his predecessors did of their own volition? Hiding something? 30 Oct 2012 13:34

The President has until tomorrow at 12 noon to pick up $5M for his favorite charity. Looking like he won't be doing it. What is he hiding? 31 Oct 2012 9:30

President Obama, please take the $5M check for charity tomorrow. It is so easy and could do so much good! 31 Oct 2012 15:45

I will soon be releasing my response to the fact that President Obama refused to show his applications and records to the public. 1 Nov 2012 11:01

It's 10 AM: Two hours to go for Obama to easily pick up millions for charity! 1 Nov 2012 8:59

Everybody knows why Obama would not show his college applications --- they are just not willing to say! 2 Nov 2012 8:57

If I would have offered Obama a billion dollars to show his records, he would have refused. 2 Nov 2012 8:56

@mcuban ---- Do you mean the President's birthplace? 5 Nov 2012 16:16

Obama thinks he can just laugh off the fact that he refuses to release his records to the American public. He can't. 6 Nov 2012 15:39

Remember: Obama turned down $5M to charity which I said I would increase by 10X to $50M--just to show simple records. He's hiding lots! 6 Nov 2012 10:33

Isn't it ironic that President Obama, of all people, is pushing for 'universal background checks?!' 27 Feb 2013 16:22

Why are people upset w/ me over Pres Obama's birth certificate?I got him to release it, or whatever it was, when nobody else could! 22 Aug 2013 15:41

People should be proud of the fact that I got Obama to release his birth certificate, which in a recent book he "miraculously" found. 22 Aug 2013 15:41

John McCain couldn't get him to release "it" and neither could Hillary Clinton—but Donald did! 22 Aug 2013 15:42

"@HoppMar: @realDonaldTrump I saw his brother in Kenya interviewed, HE may be wiser, actually." I'm so surprised his brother lives in Kenya 20 Sep 2013 0:03

How come Snowden and ObamaCare have access to all records and information but don't have even the smallest tidbits on President Obama? 30 Oct 2013 17:54

ObamaCare is a disaster and Snowden is a spy who should be executed-but if it and he could reveal Obama's records,I might become a major fan 30 Oct 2013 17:48

"If you like your healthcare plan you can keep it." = "I was born in Hawaii." 31 Oct 2013 15:03

How amazing, the State Health Director who verified copies of Obama's "birth certificate" died in plane crash today. All others lived 12 Dec 2013 16:32

"@johnnyb23390: @realDonaldTrump - the only confidentiality agreement he signed was for his real birth certificate. keep up the great work!" 14 Jan 2014 23:10

Always remember, I was the one who got Obama to release his birth certificate, or whatever that was! Hilary couldn't, McCain couldn't. 29 Jun 2014 13:42

Attention all hackers: You are hacking everything else so please hack Obama's college records (destroyed?) and check "place of birth" 6 Sep 2014 5:06

Taming the RINO

My @NewsRadio967 interview re Jeb Bush's absurd immigration comment & @Citizens_United @AFPhq Freedom Summit. 9 Apr 2014 17:15

Via @NewHampJournal by @jdistaso: "In NH 'The Donald' hammers Mitt Jeb as he again weighs a run for President" 17 Nov 2014 17:03

"Donald Trump on Jeb Bush: 'The last thing we need is another Bush'" via @fox5newsdc by @EmilyMiller 16 Dec 2014 20:00

Via @ABC by @jonkarl & @JordynPhelps: "Donald Trump Says Jeb Bush is the 'Last Thing We Need'" 17 Dec 2014 21:12

Must read @ConservReview article by @JeffJlpa1: "Jeb Bush and the Outsiders" 19 Dec 2014 15:39

Where's the electability? Jeb is losing to HRC by 13 points. A Bush will never beat a Clinton. Wake up @GOP! 30 Dec 2014 21:24

Via @NYDailyNews by Rich Schapiro: "Donald Trump slams Mitt Romney Jeb Bush" 25 Jan 2015 18:33

Donald Trump: Jeb Bush's Support of Common Core 'a Disaster' via @BreitbartNews by Dr. Susan Berry 25 Jan 2015 19:20

@Belle_2016: @greta I would vote for @realDonaldTrump for President with @marcorubio as vice president. That would work for people in Fla. 24 Mar 2015 23:22

@justariot66: Rand Cruz Rubio next week. A hat trick of never gonna win" Donald if you ever were for real this is the time." 9 Apr 2015 8:07

@MamaGlove: Please tell Cruz & Rubio we are trying to return to the Constitution.No more usurpers #RunTrumpRun #MakeAmericaGreatAgain 11 Apr 2015 3:28

Marco Rubio should pick a location that has working air conditioning next time - especially when in Miami - proper plan.

Sweating profusely! 14 Apr 2015 2:30

Jeb Bush - "I am a conservative" = Barack Obama -"If you like your healthcare plan you can keep your plan." 16 Apr 2015 20:36

Fact – while Jeb was governor & Rubio was House Majority Leader Florida's debt more than doubled. Conservatives? 23 Apr 2015 17:22

@ByronYork: In new Bloomberg poll Donald Trump ahead of Christie Cruz Carson Huckabee Fiorina Graham Jindal Kasich Perry Santorum. 12 May 2015 6:02

Jeb Bush really blew his interview with @megynkelly - should cost him big time. Said he would do the disastrous Iraq war all over again 13 May 2015 1:30

I call Jeb Bush the reluctant warrior --- he just doesn't want to be doing this he is not having fun! 14 May 2015 12:59

@GappistanRadio: Jeb Bush Marco Rubio Ted Cruz are not the answers. America needs Trump to send Hillary packing and make USA great again! 14 May 2015 13:18

Via @bostonherald by @ ChrisCassidy_BH: "Donald Trump says Jeb Bush is wrong about Iraq" 14 May 2015 19:56

I cannot believe how bad Jeb Bush looks with his insane answer on Iraq and then his numerous corrections which made him look even worse. 15 May 2015 13:02

Jeb Bush gave five different answers in four days on whether or not we should have invaded Iraq.He is so confused.Not presidential material! 18 May 2015 1:04

Marco Rubio was a complete disaster today in an interview with Chris Wallace @FoxNews concerning our invading Iraq. He was as clueless as Jeb 18 May 2015 1:11

I laugh when I see Marco Rubio and Jeb Bush pretending to "love" each other with each talking of their great friendship. Typical phony pols 18 May 2015 1:54

Marco Rubio had no idea what he was doing on Chris Wallace show. Said Iraq "was not a mistake." He looked clueless! 18 May 2015 12:15

Remember when Jeb gave Hillary a medal on the 1 year anniversary of Benghazi?! Guess he would have invaded Libya too! 19 May 2015 15:09

I now see John Kasich from Ohio- who is desperate to run- is using my line "Make America Great Again". Typical pol- no imagination! 20 May 2015 14:07

What people don't know about Kasich- he was a managing partner of the horrendous Lehman Brothers when it totally destroyed the economy! 20 May 2015 14:07

@MarcoRubioTNews: Is America ready for Donald Trump as president? Wayne Allen Root-wow great words and delivery! 21 May 2015 8:11

Politicians are all talk and no action. Bush and Rubio couldn't answer simple question on Iraq. They will NEVER make America great again! 28 May 2015 2:35

Flashback — Jeb Bush received a $4M tax payer bailout in 1990. Guess who was POTUS then? 22 Jun 2015 17:16

The highly respected Suffolk University poll just announced that I am alone in 2nd place in New Hampshire with Jeb Bust (Bush) in first. 24 Jun 2015 12:12

Just out the new nationwide @FoxNews poll has me alone in 2nd place closely behind Jeb Bush-but Bush will NEVER Make America Great Again! 25 Jun 2015 0:48

Once again the Bush appointed Supreme Court Justice John Roberts has let us down. Jeb pushed him hard! Remember! 26 Jun 2015 14:06

@tedcruz now I know you're smart! See you soon. #TCOT #MAKEAMERICAGREATAGAIN! 30 Jun 2015 20:17

.@marcorubio what do you say to the family of Kathryn Steinle in CA who was viciously killed b/c we can't secure our border? Stand up for US 3 Jul 2015 23:26

@funtravel777: @RoniSeale @usplaymoney @marcorubio Donald Trump can't be bought bullied or intimidated. He is a strong leader. 4 Jul 2015 3:47

@mariclaire81: @justdoit377 @realDonaldTrump @marcorubio I do not yet who I will vote for but can assure you it will not be Rubio 4 Jul 2015 20:55

@zengadfly: .@VRWCTexan @JebBush @marcorubio @realDonaldTrump @gatewaypundit More than a few voters may #PlayTheTrumpCard! #backlash 4 Jul 2015 22:29

Via @BreitbartNews: "GAME ON: TRUMP RESPONDS TO JEB" 4 Jul 2015 22:48

@bdean1468: @JebBush & @marcorubio couldn't carry @realDonaldTrump 's gym bags. #Trump2016 4 Jul 2015 22:50

Jeb Bush will never secure our border or negotiate great trade deals for American workers. Jeb doesn't see & can't solve the problems. 5 Jul 2015 15:02

Flashback – Jeb Bush says illegal immigrants breaking our laws is an "act of love" He will never secure the border. 5 Jul 2015 15:23

"RUBIO'S GANG OF 8 BILL WOULD HAVE REWARDED SANCTUARY CITIES HARBORING ILLEGALS" Marco is a politician-he flip flops! 7 Jul 2015 23:15

Jeb's brother George insisted on a $100000 fee and $20000 for a private jet to speak at a charity for severely wounded vets. Not nice! 9 Jul 2015 11:25

@KBrocking: @realDonaldTrump @krauthammer The Donald is the only good Republican candidate in my opinion. Rubio Perry etc??? Um no. 9 Jul 2015 12:15

Jeb Bush just announced he raised over $100M. Everyone of those people who contributed are getting something to the detriment of America! 10 Jul 2015 14:51

Can you envision Jeb Bush or Hillary Clinton negotiating with 'El Chapo' the Mexican drug lord who escaped from prison? .... 13 Jul 2015 0:25

More Bush cronyism – "Jeb Bush and the Common Core Money Trail". It's the Bush way! 16 Jul 2015 20:06

Via @AP March2013: Jeb said "he was open to...pathway for citizenship for illegal immigrants" Lying on campaign trail! 17 Jul 2015 18:09

.@tedcruz you were terrific on @seanhannity tonight. I am going to the border tomorrow. 23 Jul 2015 2:30

A nation WITHOUT BORDERS is not a nation at all. We must

have a wall. The rule of law matters. Jeb just doesn't get it. 28 Jul 2015 21:20

Via @SaintPetersblog by @MitchEPerry: "Shock poll: Donald Trump leads Jeb Bush 26-20% … in Florida" 29 Jul 2015 19:21

Despite the false @nytimes story about Jeb Bush being happy with the Trump surge he fell more than anybody & is miserable. 3 Aug 2015 15:33

@Mike_Beacham: Trump Leads Jeb Slips Rubio Crashes In WSJ/NBC News Poll #StraightTalk @SenTedCruz #ccot #tcot #2A 5 Aug 2015 1:12

Many of Hillary's donors are the same donors as Jeb Bush's—all rich will have total control—know them well. 5 Aug 2015 14:37

Do you notice that Hillary spews out Jeb's name as often as possible in order to give him status? She knows Trump is her worst nightmare. 5 Aug 2015 14:37

@TIME poll: @realDonaldTrump winner of last night's debate by wide margin.. 45% v.12% @RealBenCarson 10% @JohnKasich 7 Aug 2015 9:15

.@SenTedCruz had a very good debate far better than Rand Paul. 11 Aug 2015 2:36

Jeb Bush signed memo saying not to use the term "anchor babies" offensive. Now he wants to use it because I use it. Stay true to yourself! 21 Aug 2015 13:49

Jeb Bush is weak on illegal immigration in favor of common core bad on women's health issues and thinks the Iraq war was a good thing. 22 Aug 2015 22:19

Jeb Bush has a photoshopped photo for an ad which gives him a black left hand and much different looking body. Jeb just can't get it right! 22 Aug 2015 22:27

Via Int'l Business Times: Jeb Bush Got $1.3M Job at Lehman After Florida Shifted Pension Cash To Bank. 24 Aug 2015 18:29

Jeb Bush never uses his last name on advertising signage materials etc. Is he ashamed of the name BUSH? A pretty sad situation. Go Jeb! 25 Aug 2015 2:57

Asians are very offended that JEB said that anchor babies applies to them as a way to be more politically correct to hispanics. A mess! 25 Aug 2015 10:52

Jeb Bush just talked about my border proposal to build a "fence." It's not a fence Jeb it's a WALL and there's a BIG difference! 25 Aug 2015 12:39

@linda_lcarson: @realDonaldTrump Rubio and Bush cant say Wall. I guess it is not pc. Just like obama cant say islamic terrorists !! 25 Aug 2015 12:59

Wow Jeb Bush just lost three of his top fundraisers - they quit! 29 Aug 2015 12:45

This is no "act of love" as Jeb Bush said... 31 Aug 2015 16:23

Yet another weak hit by a candidate with a failing campaign. Will Jeb sink as low in the polls as the others who have gone after me? 1 Sep 2015 15:56

Jeb is spending millions of dollars on "hit" ads funded by lobbyists & special interests. Bad system. 1 Sep 2015 15:56

Remember that I am self-funding my campaign. Hillary Jeb and the rest are spending special interest and lobbyist money.100% CONTROLLED 5 Sep 2015 21:46

Looking forward to being with @SenTedCruz at our big rally in D.C. on Wednesday (1:00 P.M. at the Capitol) to protest insane Iran nuke deal! 7 Sep 2015 20:25

Wake up Jeb supporters! 8 Sep 2015 18:55

I'm self funding my campaign but lobbyists & special interests for Jeb & others are starting to do big ads—desperate! Don't believe them. 8 Sep 2015 19:41

The lobbyists & special interests have just put out an ad for Jeb which hits me "just a little" but is very false! 8 Sep 2015 19:41

Jeb's policies in Florida helped lead to its almost total collapse. Right after he left he went to work for Lehman Brothers—wow! 8 Sep 2015 19:44

Man did JEB throw his brother under the bus last night on @colbertlateshow . Probably true but not nice! 9 Sep 2015 19:46

Jeb has been confused for forty years- 21 Sep 2015 15:26

2016 Republican Primary Morning Consult Poll was just released. TRUMP 32 CARSON 12 BUSH 11 FIORINA 6 RUBIO 5 CRUZ 5. Taken after debate 22 Sep 2015 12:59

Headline reads" Rubio passes Bush in Florida poll" -- Unfair because Trump destroys them both! Trump 31.5% Rubio 19.2% Bush 11.3% 23 Sep 2015 15:12

Just watched @marcorubio on television. Just another all talk no action politician. Truly doesn't have a clue! Worst voting record in Sen. 25 Sep 2015 3:23

@yayala19: @marcorubio WHAT THE LOBBYISTS THE MEDIA AND CAREER POLITICIANS WILL DO NEXT TO TRY TO STOP TRUMP? SILENT MAJORITY IS BACK 25 Sep 2015 3:48

.@MarcoRubio is weak on illegal immigration and will allow anyone into the country..... 25 Sep 2015 19:18

.....Has worst attendance record in Senate- rarely there to vote on a bill! @marcorubio 25 Sep 2015 19:19

Lightweight Senator Marco Rubio is VERY weak on immigration knows nothing about finance and would be incapable of making great trade deals! 26 Sep 2015 13:03

Marco Rubio is a member of the Gang Of Eight or very weak on stopping illegal immigration. Only changed when poll numbers crashed. 26 Sep 2015 13:12

Conservative? Jeb Bush doubled Florida State debt! 28 Sep 2015 19:21

I watched lightweight Senator Marco Rubio who is all talk and no action defend his WEAK position on illegal immigration. Pathetic! 30 Sep 2015 11:24

Rubio is totally owned by the lobbyists and special interests. A lightweight senator with the worst voting record in Senate. Lazy! 30 Sep 2015 12:20

Anyone reading this profile of Marco Rubio would never vote for him. Never made ten cents & is totally controlled! 30 Sep 2015 14:59

Bush and Rubio are finally attacking each other as I knew they would in order to be the last "establishment" man standing against me. Great 3 Oct 2015 11:16

Rubio was very disloyal to Bush his mentor when he decided to run against him. Both said they "love" each other. They don't - word is hate! 3 Oct 2015 11:21

@CASuperrunner: @cu_mr2ducks @FoxNews @foxnewspolitics Trump talked about this weeks ago as a possibility .... this is not Rubio's idea 6 Oct 2015 4:00

@LarrySchweikart: @peddoc63 @RickCanton @realDonaldTrump @marcorubio Funny. The Donald living rent-free in lil Marco's head 6 Oct 2015 11:31

@AngelaDale143: @realDonaldTrump @CNN wow did Trump kick ass with Cuomo! You are the man Mr. Trump; certainly not the lamb chop Rubio. 6 Oct 2015 11:32

@darcy027027: @GardiBates @ananavarro @CNN Just In! 10/6/15 Morning Poll Trump +18% Trump 31 Carson 13 Rubio 10 Bush 7 Fiorina 6 7 Oct 2015 0:02

@3462727: @BretBaier @Norsu2 @realDonaldTrump tired of FOX bashing Trump & pushing GOP establish / Christie/Rubio/Bush 7 Oct 2015 23:21

Website Exposing Marco 'Amnesty' Rubio Goes Live: A 'Donor Class Puppet'? - Breitbart 8 Oct 2015 20:00

Sheldon Adelson is looking to give big dollars to Rubio because he feels he can mold him into his perfect little puppet. I agree! 13 Oct 2015 10:46

The arrogant young woman who questioned me in such a nasty fashion at No Labels yesterday was a Jeb staffer! HOW CAN HE BEAT RUSSIA & CHINA? 13 Oct 2015 11:39

How can Jeb Bush expect to deal with China Russia + Iran if he gets caught doing a "plant" during my speech yesterday in NH? 13 Oct 2015 15:52

@LaurenDa123: @realDonaldTrump I think @JebBush and @marcorubio are supposed to be on this stage 14 Oct 2015 1:20

CNN/ORC Poll results just out for Nevada—WOW! Trump 38 Carson 22 Fiorina 8 Bush 6 Cruz 4 14 Oct 2015 18:23

.@JebBushAt the debate you said your brother kept us safe- I wanted to be nice & did not mention the WTC came down during his watch 9/11. 17 Oct 2015 1:07

No @JebBush you're pathetic for saying nothing happened during your brother's term when the World Trade Center was attacked and came down. 17 Oct 2015 1:29

.@JebBush like it or not our country needs more energy and spirit than you can provide! #MakeAmericaGreatAgain 17 Oct 2015 1:31

Via CNET: Donald Trump Bests Jeb Bush in Website Performance Experts Say- 17 Oct 2015 16:01

Jeb Bush should stop trying to defend his brother and focus on his own shortcomings and how to fix them. Also Rubio is hitting him hard! 18 Oct 2015 13:04

Jeb why did your brother attack and destabalize the Middle East by attacking Iraq when there were no weapons of mass destruction? Bad info? 18 Oct 2015 13:29

@d_seaman: @realDonaldTrump Trump wins hands down: Jeb is weak Rubio is broke. 18 Oct 2015 15:48

@RD_2008: @JebBush Quit Jeb Quit. Your poll is even lower than your apprentice Rubio. @realDonaldTrump 18 Oct 2015 21:12

Jeb is fighting to defend a catastrophic event. I am fighting to make sure it doesn't happen again.Jeb is too soft-we need tougher & sharper 19 Oct 2015 13:36

Via @IBTimes: "Under Fire From Donald Trump Jeb Bush Focuses On 9/11 Even Though Hijackers Got Florida Licenses" 19 Oct 2015 19:21

@Portosj81J: @realDonaldTrump #Trump2016 #Trump hits his highest poll number yet; #Carson #Rubio make small gains 21 Oct 2015 0:25

Just out: Boston Herald/Franklin Pierce Poll N.H. TRUMP 28 (up 10) CARSON 16 BUSH 9 RUBIO 6 CRUZ 5 Press will say they are surging! 21 Oct 2015 10:36

Can u believe that Jeb Bush's campaign manager is in Berlin Germany looking for money? What's he giving to Germany? 21 Oct 2015 20:58

.@JebBush is totally lost -- he spends too much time managing the bloated staff of his campaign & not enough talking about America's future. 24 Oct 2015 20:42

.@JebBush had a tiny 300 person crowd at Senator Tim Scott's forum. I had thousands and they had real passion! 24 Oct 2015 20:43

.@JebBush is slashing campaign salaries people making millions. If he can't manage his campaign how can he manage our countries finances? 24 Oct 2015 20:44

While Jeb Bush is cutting staff and salaries after having paid ridiculous amounts of money why did he pay so much in the first place? 25 Oct 2015 3:24

This is just not the right time for Jeb Bush. His campaign is in total disarray too much staff being paid way too much money = U.S. GOVT. 25 Oct 2015 10:36

.@CBSNews Poll - WOW! New Hampshire TRUMP 38% CARSON 12% BUSH 8% South Carolina TRUMP 40% CARSON 23% CRUZ 8% Iowa TRUMP 27% CARSON 27% 25 Oct 2015 16:11

Remember that Carson Bush and Rubio are VERY weak on illegal immigration. They will do NOTHING to stop it. Our country will be overrun! 25 Oct 2015 20:49

Trump's National Lead Increases to 35.6% Going into the Third GOP Debate it's Trump Carson and Rubio 27 Oct 2015 16:14

@CNBC POLL TOTAL: TRUMP 25.22 CARSON 19.78 RUBIO 9.67.... 28 Oct 2015 20:10

@DRUDGE_REPORT: TRUMP WINS CNBC INSTANT POLL; RUBIO SECOND... DEVELOPING... 29 Oct 2015 14:42

@BentleyforTrump: @realDonaldTrump @DRUDGE_REPORT We need a wall not a Rubio 29 Oct 2015 15:52

@giatny: Rubio an orator/liar like Obama but totally unqualified. Rubio visa bill did NOT protect American workers. See Disney. 30 Oct 2015 14:38

When candidate John Kasich on the @oreillyfactor talked about dismantling Medicare and Medicaid he was referring to Ben Carson. 31 Oct 2015 4:20

I am going to save Medicare and Medicaid Carson wants to abolish and failing candidate Gov. John Kasich doesn't have a clue - weak! 31 Oct 2015 4:30

I see Marco Rubio just landed another billionaire to give big money to his Superpac which are total scams. Marco must address him as "SIR"! 31 Oct 2015 12:23

Gov. John Kasich has really failed on the campaign trail. I thought he would have been far more talented. He is just wasting time & money! 1 Nov 2015 2:31

@PaulaPedene: Trump Leads GOP Carson Stays Strong Rubio 3rd: Poll 1 Nov 2015 2:48

Further proof that Gang of Eight member Marco Rubio is weak on illegal immigration is Paul Singer's Mr. Amnesty endorsement.Rubs can't win 1 Nov 2015 12:29

Anybody that believes in strong borders and stopping illegal immigration cannot vote for Marco Rubio READ THIS: 1 Nov 2015 12:40

Jeb's new slogan - "Jeb can fix it". I never thought of Jeb as a crook! Stupid message the word "fix" is not a good one to use in politics! 1 Nov 2015 13:48

I told you in speeches months ago that Jeb and Marco do not like each other. Marco is too ambitious and very disloyal to Jeb as his mentor! 1 Nov 2015 13:52

Marco Rubio will not win. Weak on illegal immigration strong on amnesty and has the appearance to killers of the world as a "lightweight". 1 Nov 2015 13:58

If Jeb Bush were more competent he could not have lost the skirmish with Marco in the debate. BAD facts for Marco if properly delivered! 1 Nov 2015 14:03

@kingster73: @realDonaldTrump Rubio is irresponsible on finances and doesn't show up for work! Who would hire him? Not the American People! 3 Nov 2015 1:38

.@CharlesGKoch is looking for a new puppet after Governor Walker and Jeb Bush cratered. He now likes Rubio--next fail. 3 Nov 2015 14:49

Jeb Bush just said about Marco Rubio "he's my friend!" Pure political speak. Why can't he be truthful and say "disloyal guy no friend!" 5 Nov 2015 9:00

.@seanhannity should have corrected Jeb Bush when he said that I "ran for president twice." Never ran merely considered running! 5 Nov 2015 9:17

Rubio lied about my meeting w/ Hispanic activists. I didn't change my opinion but treated them w/ respect. Shame! 5 Nov 2015 23:30

@GrundleMan27: Marco Rubio can't even handle his own credit card how is he going to be able to handle the U.S. finances #trump 6 Nov 2015 9:54

@rhinostate: .@realDonaldTrump @GrundleMan27 Rubio is a Manchurian Candidate. People will own him if he ever became president. 6 Nov 2015 9:59

Florida Ethics Commission Advocate comes down hard on Rubio. So do two people who worked with him. Said he used the wrong credit card! Sure. 6 Nov 2015 11:58

@JimmyForTrump: @insighter007 @OAmericanGirl All Rep should stand with #Trump2016 Forget Bush Rubio and knife attackers! #Trump2016 6 Nov 2015 16:41

@Watchman4the1: Chuck Schumer: Sen Marco Rubio Is "Totally Committed To Obama's Immigration Agenda" DonaldTrump 8 Nov 2015 22:48

@DRUDGE_REPORT: REUTERS 5-DAY ROLLING POLL: TRUMP 34% CARSON 19.6% RUBIO 9.7% CRUZ 7.7%... Thank you - a great honor! 13 Nov 2015 19:42

.@CarlyFiorina Carly not just you I also told Gov. Kasich to "let Jeb talk give him a chance" because Kasich was constantly cutting in. 13 Nov 2015 20:16

@tasteofaz: Poll: Trump Surges to 42% Nationally; 'Bad News for Marco Rubio' @realdonaldtrump Great news! 15 Nov 2015 4:00

@FoxNews New Hampshire Poll: @realDonaldTrump 'Rules GOP Race in New Hampshire.' Trump 27 Rubio 13 Cruz 11 Bush 9 Carson 9 & Kasich 7 18 Nov 2015 23:53

Governor Kasich whose failed campaign & debating skills have brought him way down in the polls is going to spend $2.5 million against me. 20 Nov 2015 1:04

John Kasich should focus his special interest money on building up his failed image not negative ads on me. 20 Nov 2015 1:05

John Kasich despite being Governor of Ohio is losing to me in the Ohio polls. Pathetic! 20 Nov 2015 1:05

I want to do negative ads on John Kasich but he is so irrelevant to the race that I don't want to waste my money. 20 Nov 2015 1:05

Watch Kasich squirm --- if he is not truthful in his negative ads I will sue him just for fun! 20 Nov 2015 1:06

Kasich has already spent $6 million on ads in New Hampshire and his numbers have gone down. People from NH are smart! 20 Nov 2015 1:06

I loved beating John Kasich in the debates but it was easy— he came in dead last! 20 Nov 2015 1:06

Doesn't help Kasich to do negative ads on me because he still has to go through everyone else - he's almost last. 20 Nov 2015 1:06

John Kasich fell right into President Obama's trap on ObamaCare and the people of Ohio are suffering for it. Shame! 20 Nov 2015 1:06

Once John Kasich announced he was running for president and opened his mouth people realized he was a complete & total dud! 20 Nov 2015 1:47

John Kasich was managing director of Lehman Brothers when it crashed bringing down the world and ruining people's lives. A total failure! 20 Nov 2015 1:55

Rumor has it - Pataki Kasich & Senator Lindsey Graham are dropping out of the race very soon. Hope it's not true they're so easy to beat! 21 Nov 2015 15:35

Going to Ohio home of one of the worst presidential candidates in history--Kasich. Can't debate loves #ObamaCare-- dummy! 23 Nov 2015 22:11

@AnnCoulter: If you run anyone but Trump Hillary wins. So Rubio Christie Jeb! & Kasich must hate the country. 24 Nov 2015 21:13

What is Frank VanderSloot getting for agreeing to back Marco Rubio? Last victim was Mitt Romney - see how that turned out. 24 Nov 2015 22:03

@nobaddog: @RepBJNikkel @CindyBlackwel12 JohnKasich All you career Politicians are shaking in your shoes for fear Trump gets elected 28 Nov 2015 23:10

@Barber2012Jeff: @realDonaldTrump John Kasich-it didn't work I'm still voting for #Trump John has done so poorly in the debates he's done! 30 Nov 2015 2:57

.@JRubinBlogger one of the dumber bloggers @washingtonpost only writes purposely inaccurate pieces on me. She is in love with Marco Rubio? 4 Dec 2015 20:37

@dr_tweedy: @CNN @JohnKasich Kasick message is as muddled and stagnant as his political career. Lied about Trump crowd. Media-he LIED! 6 Dec 2015 14:52

@CindyBlackwel12:   @dr_tweedy @CNN @JohnKasich AMERICA WANTS #TRUMP @jaketapper   Politicians are so dishonest! 6 Dec 2015 15:19

@BrianBl43802294 @JohnKasich Trump is not controlled by donorsspecial interestsLobbyists like U.Ur a total puppet. Trump is working 4 U.S. 6 Dec 2015 17:49

Poor @JohnKasich doesn't have what it takes- 7 Dec 2015 17:29

Just won IOWA @CNN Poll BIG: Trump 33% Cruz 20% Rubio 11% but @WSJ reported "Cruz momentum" but nothing about the fact that I easily won! 8 Dec 2015 14:25

Thank you @JebBush- you finally get it! 9 Dec 2015 18:46

Looks like @tedcruz is getting ready to attack. I am leading by so much he must. I hope so he will fall like all others. Will be easy! 11 Dec 2015 12:49

.@tedcruz should not make statements behind closed doors to his bosses he should bring them out into the open - more fun that way! 11 Dec 2015 12:53

John Podesta says nominee will be Cruz b/c last person Hillary wants to face is Trump! Use your head folks! 46-41! 12 Dec 2015 19:13

New CNN Iowa poll --- Trump 33 Cruz 20. Everyone else way down! Don't trust Des Moines Register poll- biased towards Trump! 12 Dec 2015 22:56

I was disappointed that Ted Cruz would speak behind my back get caught and then deny it. Well welcome to the wonderful world of politics! 13 Dec 2015 22:31

Why doesn't @FoxNews quote the new Iowa @CNN Poll where I have a 33% to 20% lead over Ted Cruz and all others. Think about it! 14 Dec 2015 5:55

Isn't it amazing that @CNN paid a fortune for an Iowa Poll which shows me in first place over Cruz by 13% 33% to 20% - then doesn't use it 15 Dec 2015 14:47

.@megynkelly is very bad at math. She was totally unable to figure out the difference between me and Cruz in the new Monmouth Poll 41to14. 15 Dec 2015 15:34

Jeb Bush had a tough night at the debate. Now he'll probably take some of his special interest money he is their puppet and buy ad's. 16 Dec 2015 15:20

I have an idea for @JebBush whose campaign is a disaster. Try using your last name & don't be ashamed of it! 18 Dec 2015 18:25

Weak & ineffective @JebBush is doing ads where he shows his statement in the debate but not my response. False advertising! 18 Dec 2015 19:50

.@JebBush has embarrassed himself & his family with his incompetent campaign for President. He should remain true to himself. 18 Dec 2015 20:43

.@JebBush was terrible on Face The Nation today. Being at 2% and falling seems to have totally affected his confidence. A basket case! 20 Dec 2015 23:13

.@JebBush today said he didn't want to be the front-runner he would rather be where he is now 2%. That is the talk of a loser can't win! 21 Dec 2015 4:42

Weak and low energy @JebBush whose campaign is a disaster is now doing ads against me where he tries to look like a tough guy. 22 Dec 2015 21:19

.@JebBush just took millions of $'s in special interest money to look like a tough guy. Will never work! 22 Dec 2015 21:20

Will @JebBush in his phony advertising campaign show himself asking me to apologize to his wife in the debate? 22 Dec 2015 21:22

Why doesn't @JebBush in his ads show my answer to his statement in the debate? 22 Dec 2015 21:23

.@JebBush's opening and closing in the debate were said by all to be terrible--fumbled around incoherent. 22 Dec 2015 21:25

Jeb's big ad buy against me paid for by lobbyists shows my face but doesn't have me answering Jeb's statements. He is really pathetic! 22 Dec 2015 22:50

Wow new Reuters Poll just out. Big lead if you want to MAKE AMERICA GREAT AGAIN! TRUMP 37 CRUZ 11 This is at the top of Drudge! 23 Dec 2015 2:59

Big news just out - NEW @CNN POLL TRUMP 39 and leads in every major category. Likeability way up. CRUZ 18 CARSON 10 RUBIO 10 23 Dec 2015 12:02

The @washingtonpost which is the lobbyist (power) for not imposing taxes on #Amazon today did a nasty cartoon attacking @tedcruz kids. Bad 23 Dec 2015 14:55

Poor @JebBush spent $50 million on his campaign I spent almost nothing. He's bottom (and gone) I'm top (by a lot). That's what U.S. needs! 24 Dec 2015 20:10

In the ridiculous @JebBush ad about me Jeb is speaking to me during the debate but doesn't allow my answer which destroys him - SO SAD! 24 Dec 2015 22:14

Wow even lowly Rand Paul has just past @JebBush in the new @CNN Poll. Jeb is at 3% I'm at 39%. Stop throwing your money down the drain! 24 Dec 2015 22:20

.@meetthepress and @chucktodd very dishonest in not showing the new @CNN Poll where I am at 39% 21points higher than Cruz. Be honest Chuck! 24 Dec 2015 23:04

Remember when failed candidate @JebBush said that illegals came across the border as AN ACT OF LOVE? He's spent $59 million and is at 3%. 25 Dec 2015 20:24

@Sir_Max: andreajmarkley: Rubio finally gets an endorsement – from #Benghazi loser Gowdy #Tcot #pjnet 27 Dec 2015 12:37

So I have spent almost nothing on my run for president and am in 1st place. Jeb Bush has spent $59 million & done. Run country my way! 29 Dec 2015 14:39

I hope @TGowdySC does better for Rubio than he did at the #Benghazi hearings which were a total disaster for Republicans & America! 29 Dec 2015 20:36

.@JebBush has spent $63000000 and is at the bottom of the polls. I have spent almost nothing and am at the top. WIN! @hughhewitt 31 Dec 2015 5:10

People ask "why do you tweet and re-tweet to millions about @JebBush when he is so low in the polls?" Because of his big $ hit ads on me! 31 Dec 2015 10:04

@whispers34: Nevada Poll: Donald Trump 33% Ted Cruz 20% Marco Rubio 11%... via @thelastrefuge2 Great news! 31 Dec 2015 11:01

I would feel sorry for @JebBush and how badly he is doing with his campaign other than for the fact he took millions of $'s of hit ads on me 31 Dec 2015 15:07

.@JebBush is a sad case. A total embarrassment to both himself and his family he just announced he will continue to spend on Trump hit ads! 2 Jan 2016 12:10

.@JebBush is a low energy "stiff" who should focus his special interest money on the many people ahead of him in the polls. Has no chance! 2 Jan 2016 12:17

Hillary Clinton doesn't have the strength or stamina to be president. Jeb Bush is a low energy individual but Hillary is not much better! 2 Jan 2016 20:00

Woody Johnson owner of the NYJets is @JebBush's finance chairman. If Woody would've been w/me he would've been in the playoffs at least! 4 Jan 2016 20:00

It was a very wise move that Ted Cruz renounced his Canadian citizenship 18 months ago. Senator John McCain is certainly no friend of Ted! 7 Jan 2016 11:28

.@SenTedCruz Ted--free legal advice on how to pre-empt the

Dems on citizen issue. Go to court now & seek Declaratory Judgment--you will win! 7 Jan 2016 16:14

I have an idea for @JebBush whose campaign is a disaster. Try using your last name and don't be ashamed of it! 7 Jan 2016 16:26

Weak & ineffective @JebBush is doing ads where he shows his statement in the debate but not my response. False advertising! 7 Jan 2016 16:30

@LiberatedCit: @JebBush Key State Florida Poll: Trump 32% Beats #Rubio-#Bush Combined 8 Jan 2016 3:29

Hank Greenberg formerly of AIG gave $10 million to the @JebBush campaign 3 months ago. He is not happy a total waste of money! 8 Jan 2016 15:57

Not good news for Jeb Bush 8 Jan 2016 18:47

Just found out that @tedcruz is spending a fortune on Iowa push polls negative to me. Not nice but OK! New polls are great. 13 Jan 2016 4:25

Sadly there is no way that Ted Cruz can continue running in the Republican Primary unless he can erase doubt on eligibility. Dems will sue! 13 Jan 2016 14:26

RT @DRUDGE_REPORT: REUTERS ROLLING: TRUMP 39% CRUZ 14.5% BUSH 10.6% CARSON 9.6% RUBIO 6.7%... MORE... 13 Jan 2016 18:23

Jeb Bush who did poorly last night in the debate and whose chances of winning are zero just got Graham endorsement. Graham quit at 0. 15 Jan 2016 15:17

Ted Cruz was born in Canada and was a Canadian citizen until 15 months ago. Lawsuits have just been filed with more to follow. I told you so 16 Jan 2016 11:40

Ted Cruz said he "didn't know" that he was a Canadian Citizen. He also FORGOT to file his Goldman Sachs Million $ loan papers.Not believable 16 Jan 2016 11:49

Was there another loan that Ted Cruz FORGOT to file. Goldman Sachs owns him he will do anything they demand. Not much of a reformer! 16 Jan 2016 11:52

The Ted Cruz wiseguy apology to the people of New York is

a disgrace. Remember his wife's employer and his lender is located there! 16 Jan 2016 12:12

Oh no just reported that Ted Cruz didn't report another loan this one from Citi. Wow no wonder banks do so well in the U.S. Senate. 16 Jan 2016 12:17

Based on the fact that Ted Cruz was born in Canada and is therefore a "natural born Canadian" did he borrow unreported loans from C banks? 16 Jan 2016 12:23

Ted Cruz purposely and illegally did not list on his personal disclosure form personally guaranteed loans from banks. They own him! 16 Jan 2016 13:31

If Ted Cruz is so opposed to gay marriage why did he accept money from people who espouse gay marriage? 16 Jan 2016 18:21

Everybody that loves the people of New York and all they have been thru should get hypocrites like Ted Cruz out of politics! 16 Jan 2016 18:22

When will @TedCruz give all the New York based campaign contributions back to the special interests that control him. 16 Jan 2016 18:23

Greatly dishonest of @TedCruz to file a financial disclosure form & not list his lending banks- then pretend he is going to clean up Wall St 16 Jan 2016 18:26

Wow! Ted Cruz received $487K in campaign contributions $11M from a NY hedge fund mogul & $1M low int. loan from Goldman Sachs. Hypocrite 16 Jan 2016 19:32

Is this the New York that Ted Cruz is talking about & demeaning? 16 Jan 2016 19:39

I am self-funding my campaign - putting up my own money not controlled. Cruz is spending $millions on ads paid for by his N.Y. bosses. 17 Jan 2016 21:05

Just a reminder that Ted Cruz supported liberal Justice John Roberts who gave us #Obamacare. 18 Jan 2016 14:50

Ted Cruz is falling in the polls. He is nervous. People are worried about his place of birth and his failure to report his loans from banks! 19 Jan 2016 1:50

I don't think Ted Cruz can even run for President until he can assure Republican voters that being born in Canada is not a problem. Doubt! 19 Jan 2016 1:57

.@TheBrodyFile Exclusive: @realDonaldTrump Says He Will Protect Evangelicals Better Than @tedcruz #CBNNews #2016 19 Jan 2016 2:36

Wow new polls just out have Trump up and Cruz down - he is a nervous wreck! 19 Jan 2016 12:50

.@tedcruz Conflicting Stances on Birthright Citizenship [14th Amendment] Gives #TeamTrump credit. 19 Jan 2016 14:18

In the just released SC poll I increased my lead by 4 points since last poll by same firm. Up by 14! Cruz dropped 3. 19 Jan 2016 16:19

Wow the highly respected Governor of Iowa just stated that "Ted Cruz must be defeated." Big shoker! People do not like Ted. 19 Jan 2016 18:47

Bob Dole Warns of 'Cataclysmic' Losses With Ted Cruz and Says Donald Trump Would Do Better via New York Times: 20 Jan 2016 23:40

Wacko @glennbeck is a sad answer to the @SarahPalinUSA endorsement that Cruz so desperately wanted. Glenn is a failing crying lost soul! 21 Jan 2016 13:42

Sad sack @JebBush has just done another ad on me with special interest money saying I won't beat Hillary - I WILL. But he can't beat me. 21 Jan 2016 14:19

Low energy candidate @JebBush has wasted $80 million on his failed presidential campaign. Millions spent on me. He should go home and relax! 21 Jan 2016 14:32

Ted Cruz complains about my views on eminent domain but without it we wouldn't have roads highways airports schools or even pipelines. 22 Jan 2016 13:34

#TedCruz eligibility to be President not settled law says Cruz' Constitutional Law Professor #LaurenceTribe 22 Jan 2016 13:41

Highly respected Constitutional law professor Mary Brigid McManamon has just stated "Ted Cruz is not eligible to be President." Big problem 22 Jan 2016 13:54

@MiamiNewTimes: Poll: Trump has more support in Florida than Rubio and Bush combined. 22 Jan 2016 14:10

After spending $89 million @JebBush is at the bottom of the barrel in polls. He is ashamed to use the name "Bush" in ads. Low energy guy! 22 Jan 2016 15:42

Wow! New National Zogby Poll just out:.TRUMP 45. CRUZ 13. RUBIO 8. Big numbers. 22 Jan 2016 23:08

Ted Cruz went down big in just released Reuters poll - what's going on? Is it Goldman Sachs/Citi loans or Canada? 22 Jan 2016 23:58

Just watched Jeb's ad where he desperately needed mommy to help him. Jeb --- mom can't help you with ISIS the Chinese or with Putin. 23 Jan 2016 1:02

Cruz says I supported TARP which gave $25 million to Goldman Sachs the bank which loaned him the money he didn't disclose. Puppet! 23 Jan 2016 1:34

Cruz did not renounce his Canadian citizenship as a US Senator- only when he started to run for #POTUS. He could be Canadian Prime Minister. 23 Jan 2016 2:04

Is Cruz honest? He is in bed w/ Wall St. & is funded by Goldman Sachs/Citi low interest loans. No legal disclosure & never sold off assets. 23 Jan 2016 2:08

Ted Cruz poll numbers are down big. Because he was born in Canada and was until recently a Canadian citizen many believe he cannot run! 23 Jan 2016 15:07

Serious doubt in Illinois as to whether or not Cruz can run for President. First of many challenges. 24 Jan 2016 1:20

RT @JoeNBC: Trump +15 on Cruz in 2 weeks. Cruz may look back and ask why he ever attacked Trump. DT has killed him ever since. 24 Jan 2016 22:14

@Rketeltas: Rubio isn't experienced enough to be Commander in Chief. Rubio is a carbon copy of Obama. We need a true leader Vote Trump 25 Jan 2016 4:08

It's time for Ted Cruz to either settle his problem with the FACT that he was born in Canada and was a citizen of Canada or get out of race 25 Jan 2016 13:26

Ted Cruz is a nervous wreck. He is making reckless charges not caring for the truth! His poll #'s are way down! 25 Jan 2016 22:00

Cruz going down fast in recent polls- dropping like a rock. Lies never work! 25 Jan 2016 22:02

Cruz lies are almost as bad as Jeb's. These politicians will do anything to stay at the trough! 25 Jan 2016 22:04

Do you think @SenTedCruz knows about @bobvanderplaats dealings? Actually I doubt it! 26 Jan 2016 18:40

Even though I beat him in the first six debates especially the last one Ted Cruz wants to debate me again. Can we do it in Canada? 27 Jan 2016 19:33

Tennessee GOP Poll Trump 32.7%Cruz 16.5%Carson 6.6%Rubio 5.3%Christie 2.4%Jeb 1.6% 28 Jan 2016 17:51

I hear that @SenTedCruz's $$ man Robert Mercer a good man is very angry because Cruz lied to him about liquidating his (Ted's) holdings.? 28 Jan 2016 19:52

Amazing that Ted Cruz can't even get a Senator like @BenSasse who is easy to endorse him. Not one Senator is endorsing Canada Ted! 30 Jan 2016 1:25

The Cruz campaign issued a dishonest and deceptive get out the vote ad calling voters "in violation." They are now under investigation. Bad! 31 Jan 2016 12:22

.@bobvanderplaats is a total phony and dishonest guy. Asked me for expensive hotel rooms free (and more). I said pay and he endorsed Cruz! 31 Jan 2016 12:31

.@bobvanderplaats is a total phony and con man. When I wouldn't give him free hotel rooms and much more he endorsed Cruz. @foxandfriends 31 Jan 2016 12:42

Ted Cruz is totally unelectable if he even gets to run (born in Canada). Will loose big to Hillary. Polls show I beat Hillary easily! WIN! 31 Jan 2016 13:06

Ted Cruz is in trouble for not reporting his bank borrowing in his very important Financial Disclosure Form. Very low interest loans scam! 31 Jan 2016 13:16

Wow just saw an ad - Cruz is lying on so many levels. There

is nobody more against ObamaCare than me will repeal & replace. He lies! 31 Jan 2016 14:22

Because I was told I could not do well in Iowa I spent very little there - a fraction of Cruz & Rubio. Came in a strong second. Great honor 2 Feb 2016 16:14

RT @IngrahamAngle: The #CruzCrew prevailed! Smart for @MarcoRubio to keep his speech short & sweet. Ditto for @realDonaldTrump who was brie... 2 Feb 2016 18:55

RT @JoeNBC: Remarkable how cost-effective Post says Trump campaign was per vote and stunning how much Jeb spent per vote. 2 Feb 2016 19:22

Anybody who watched all of Ted Cruz's far too long rambling overly flamboyant speech last nite would say that was his Howard Dean moment! 2 Feb 2016 20:02

Ted Cruz didn't win Iowa he stole it. That is why all of the polls were so wrong and why he got far more votes than anticipated. Bad! 3 Feb 2016 13:47

During primetime of the Iowa Caucus Cruz put out a release that @RealBenCarson was quitting the race and to caucus (or vote) for Cruz. 3 Feb 2016 13:56

Many people voted for Cruz over Carson because of this Cruz fraud. Also Cruz sent out a VOTER VIOLATION certificate to thousands of voters. 3 Feb 2016 14:07

The Voter Violation certificate gave poor marks to the unsuspecting voter(grade of F) and told them to clear it up by voting for Cruz. Fraud 3 Feb 2016 14:10

And finally Cruz strongly told thousands of caucusgoers (voters) that Trump was strongly in favor of ObamaCare and "choice" - a total lie! 3 Feb 2016 14:21

Based on the fraud committed by Senator Ted Cruz during the Iowa Caucus either a new election should take place or Cruz results nullified. 3 Feb 2016 14:28

This was sent out from Ted Cruz- as Iowans arrived at their caucus sites to vote. #CruzFraud 3 Feb 2016 19:20

The State of Iowa should disqualify Ted Cruz from the most recent election on the basis that he cheated- a total fraud! 3 Feb 2016 19:25

Cruz just lied again- I am and have been totally against #ObamaCare- repeal and replace! 3 Feb 2016 20:22

Dr. Ben Carson blasted Ted Cruz for "deceit and dirty tricks and lies." 3 Feb 2016 20:44

Thank you @billoreilly & @KarlRove. Ted Cruz should be immediately disqualified in Iowa with each candidate moving up one notch. 4 Feb 2016 6:33

#ICYMI: @KarlRove & @oreillyfactor discuss what Ted Cruz did to the great people of Iowa- as they went to vote. 4 Feb 2016 6:35

.@oreillyfactor @KarlRove- as per the show an even more serious Cruz charge is the fraudulent voter violation certificate sent to everyone. 4 Feb 2016 6:36

This is the Cruz voter violation certificate sent to everyone a misdemeanor at minimum. 4 Feb 2016 6:38

Wow Jeb Bush whose campaign is a total disaster had to bring in mommy to take a slap at me. Not nice! 6 Feb 2016 14:37

@Enlighten2881: @ukcatwoman52 @ericnlin @AC360 How come Rubio&Cruz are going to turn America around but did nothing in the Senate for USA? 6 Feb 2016 17:57

@big_carsonrocks: AMERICA...Stop being duped...WAKE UP Cruz & Rubio establishment phonies. DonaldTrump only truthful & not owned candidate 6 Feb 2016 19:10

@paintonmyjeans: If I owned a big company that was failing I'd hire DonaldTrump to make it great again-Rubio/Cruz wouldnt be considered 6 Feb 2016 19:41

@MarkHalperin: My debate report card: Christie A- Trump A- Bush B+ Kasich B+ Cruz B Carson C Rubio D. Full report cards here. 7 Feb 2016 10:24

@JoeNBC: Latest UMass Tracking Poll. NH GOP Trump 35 (+1) Rubio 14 (-1) Cruz 13 (-1) Jeb 10 (+2) Kasich 10 (+2) 7 Feb 2016 10:35

@JoeNBC: Trump Kasich Jeb and Christie all had good nights. 7 Feb 2016 10:37

Jeb Bush has zero communication skills so he spent a fortune of special interest money on a Super Bowl ad. He is a weak candidate! 8 Feb 2016 12:20

Jeb Bush is desperate - strongly in favor of #CommonCore and very weak on illegal immigration. 8 Feb 2016 16:33

Everybody is laughing at Jeb Bush-spent $100 million and is at bottom of pack. A pathetic figure! 8 Feb 2016 16:38

RT @foxandfriends: "Jeb is a weak guy." @EricTrump 8 Feb 2016 18:35

Remember @JebBush wants COMMON CORE (education from D.C.) and is very weak on ILLEGAL IMMIGRATION ("come as act of love"). Not a leader! 9 Feb 2016 12:00

I know the "Governors" and Jeb Bush who has gone nasty with lies is by far the weakest of the lot. His family used private eminent domain! 9 Feb 2016 12:08

So funny Jeb Bush called me a "highly gifted politician and a great entertainer" - I assume that is a compliment! 10 Feb 2016 15:22

I was referring to the fact that Jeb Bush wants to keep common core. 11 Feb 2016 1:34

Jeb Bush spent more than $40000000 in New Hampshire to come in 4 or 5 I spent $3000000 to come in 1st. Big difference in capability! 11 Feb 2016 15:11

Jeb failed as Jeb! He gave up and enlisted Mommy and his brother (who got us into the quicksand of Iraq). Spent $120 million.Weak-no chance! 11 Feb 2016 19:45

We are getting reports from many voters that the Cruz people are back to doing very sleazy and dishonest "pushpolls" on me. We are watching! 11 Feb 2016 20:39

Cruz caught cold in lie after denial of push polls like lies w/ @RealBenCarson. How can he preach Christian values? 12 Feb 2016 0:44

Weak JEB getting thrown out by management during speech. Do you think he will be this tough on Putin & others? 12 Feb 2016 4:10

Lying Cruz put out a statement "Trump & Rubio are w/Obama on gay marriage." Cruz is the worst liar crazy or very dishonest. Perhaps all 3? 12 Feb 2016 4:20

How can Ted Cruz be an Evangelical Christian when he lies so much and is so dishonest? 12 Feb 2016 12:03

Lightweight @JebBush is spending a fortune of special interest against me in SC. False advertising- desperate and sad! 12 Feb 2016 18:59

If @TedCruz doesn't clean up his act stop cheating & doing negative ads I have standing to sue him for not being a natural born citizen. 12 Feb 2016 19:45

Last time lightweight @JebBush tried to knock off @marcorubio he made a total fool of himself. If he doesn't do better this time he is out! 12 Feb 2016 20:30

Millions of $'s of false ads paid for by lobbyists-special interests of cheater @SenTedCruz and sleepy @JebBush are now running in S.C. 12 Feb 2016 21:54

Nasty Ted Cruz is at it again- same dirty tricks he used w/ @RealBenCarson- saying I may not be on ballot & I hold liberal positions. LIES! 14 Feb 2016 0:11

Ted Cruz is a cheater! He holds the Bible high and then lies and misrepresents the facts! 14 Feb 2016 0:13

Lightweight @JebBush said tonight he didn't know his family used private eminent domain in Texas- Lie! #GOPDebate 14 Feb 2016 5:24

How can @JebBush beat Hillary Clinton- if he can't beat anyone else on the #GOPDebate stage with $150M? I am the only one who can! 14 Feb 2016 5:37

This shows what a complete & total liar Ted Cruz is- he said he wouldn't have nominated John Roberts. Really? 14 Feb 2016 14:50

Ted Cruz along with Jeb Bush pushed Justice John Roberts onto the Supreme Court. Roberts could have killed ObamaCare twice but didn't! 14 Feb 2016 22:02

Funny that Jeb(!) didn't want help from his family in his failed campaign and didn't even want to use his last name.Then mommy now brother! 15 Feb 2016 11:05

Jeb Bush and Ted Cruz are not electable presidential candidates Hillary would destroy them. Ted may not be eligible to run - born in Canada 15 Feb 2016 12:24

Now that George Bush is campaigning for Jeb(!) is he fair game for questions about World Trade Center Iraq War and eco collapse? Careful! 15 Feb 2016 14:04

I'd like to call JEB a liar but the truth is he has no clue & never revealed that he used Eminent Domain- when criticizing me! (1/2) 15 Feb 2016 17:24

Jeb used Eminent Domain & took advantage of a disabled vet in the process. (2/2) 15 Feb 2016 17:24

JEB is a hypocrite! Used massive private "Eminent Domain" --- Just another clueless politician! 15 Feb 2016 17:29

RESPONSE TO THE LIES OF SENATOR CRUZ: #Trump2016 #VoteTrumpSC 15 Feb 2016 20:23

New PPP Poll just out - Trump up big Cruz Rubio and Bush down. The debate results even with a stacked RNC audience were wonderful! 16 Feb 2016 11:22

Just out Nevada poll shows Jeb Bush at 1% he should take his dumb mouthpiece @LindseyGrahamSC and just go home. 17 Feb 2016 16:10

Jeb Bush just got contact lenses and got rid of the glasses. He wants to look cool but it's far too late. 1% in Nevada! 17 Feb 2016 16:11

I agree with Marco Rubio that Ted Cruz is a liar! 18 Feb 2016 14:11

Remember Cruz and Bush gave us Roberts who upheld #ObamaCare twice! I am the only one who will #MAKEAMERICAGREATAGAIN! 19 Feb 2016 20:30

Lying #Ted Cruz just (on election day) came out with a sneak and sleazy Robocall. He holds up the Bible but in fact is a true lowlife pol! 20 Feb 2016 13:59

@FamilyRedsFans: @FoxNews is really starting to campaign hard for marcorubio. #fairandbalancedmyass He is weak on illegal immigration! 20 Feb 2016 14:04

@ResisTyr: Mr.Trump...BOTH Cruz AND Rubio are ineligible to be POTUS! It's a SLAM DUNK CASE!! Check it! 20 Feb 2016 14:07

Remember that Marco Rubio is very weak on illegal immigration. South Carolina needs strength as illegals and Syrians pour in. Don't allow it 20 Feb 2016 17:02

A quote was read from a parody account last night on MSNBC re: Jeb. 21 Feb 2016 15:57

A number of months ago I was not expected to win South CarolinaTed Cruz was and yet I won in a landslide - every group and category. WIN! 22 Feb 2016 12:22

The reason that Ted Cruz lost the Evangelicals in S.C. is because he is a world class LIAR and Evangelicals do not like liars! 22 Feb 2016 13:36

@gregusp61: You really rocked them hard in S.C. Rubio and Cruz were pummeled. So glad Jeb is gone! Next no liar! 22 Feb 2016 13:41

@1sonny12: @KSmith233035 @mitchellvii FLORIDIANS ARE UPSET BECAUSE RUBIO DID NOT DO WHAT HE PROMISED ONCE HE WAS ELECTED! VOTE TRUMP 22 Feb 2016 13:42

It is so important to audit The Federal Reserve and yet Ted Cruz missed the vote on the bill that would allow this to be done. 22 Feb 2016 20:37

Wow Ted Cruz falsely suggested Marco Rubio mocked the Bible and was just forced to fire his Communications Director. More dirty tricks! 22 Feb 2016 20:44

Ted Cruz has been playing an ad about me that is so ridiculously false - no basis in fact. Take ad down Ted. Biggest liar in politics! 22 Feb 2016 20:50

Ted Cruz has now apologized to Marco Rubio and Ben Carson for fraud and dirty tricks. No wonder he has lost Evangelical support! 22 Feb 2016 20:55

Just saw the phony ad by Cruz - totally false more dirty tricks. He got caught in so many lies - is this man crazy? 22 Feb 2016 21:06

Ted Cruz should be disqualified from his fraudulent win in Iowa. Weak RNC and Republican leadership probably won't let this happen! Sad. 22 Feb 2016 21:11

Thank you Illinois! Great news! #VoteTrumpIL on 3/15!Trump 28%Cruz 15%Rubio 14%Kasich 13%Bush 8%Carson 6%Simon Poll/SIU 23 Feb 2016 1:24

Great poll! Thank you North Carolina! #VoteTrumpNC on 3/15!Trump 36%Cruz 18%Rubio 18%Carson 10%Kasich 7%Via @SurveyUSA 23 Feb 2016 1:34

Thank you Michigan! #VoteTrumpMITrump 35%Kasich 17%Cruz 12%Rubio 12%Carson 9% Via: ARG 23 Feb 2016 1:37

Ted Cruz said on @oreillyfactor that illegals sent out of country by my administration would come right back as citizens. Another lie-crazy! 23 Feb 2016 2:31

Ted Cruz only talks tough on immigration now because he did so badly in S.C. He is in favor of amnesty and weak on illegal immigration. 23 Feb 2016 14:37

Wow was Ted Cruz disloyal to his very capable director of communication. He used him as a scape goat-fired like a dog! Ted panicked. 23 Feb 2016 14:40

Ted Cruz does not have the right "temperment" to be President. Look at the way he totally panicked in firing his director of comm. BAD! 23 Feb 2016 15:07

Ted Cruz lifts the Bible high into the air and then lies like a dog-over and over again! The Evangelicals in S.C. figured him out & said no! 23 Feb 2016 15:15

Great. Just reported on @FoxNews that many people who supported @JebBush are now supporting me. I knew that would happen pundits didn't! 23 Feb 2016 18:12

Make sure you get on the Trump line and are not mislead by the Cruz people. They are bad! BE CAREFUL. 24 Feb 2016 2:00

Big defeat last night in Nevada for Ted Cruz and Marco Rubio. @KarlRove on @FoxNews is working hard to belittle my victory. Rove is sick! 24 Feb 2016 16:09

The polls show that I picked up many Jeb Bush supporters. That is how I got to 46%. When others drop out I will pick up more. Sad but true 24 Feb 2016 21:36

Why would Texans vote for "liar" Ted Cruz when he was born in Canada lived there for 4 years-and remained a Canadian citizen until recently 24 Feb 2016 23:45

When Ted Cruz quits the race and the field begins to clear I will get most of his votes - no problem! 24 Feb 2016 23:49

Ted Cruz is lying again. Polls are showing that I do beat Hillary Clinton head to head. Check out Poll snd Q Poll. 25 Feb 2016 2:20

@HosierN: @foxnewspolitics A vote for @tedcruz or @marcorubio is a vote for corruption special interests and lobbyists. Trump for POTUS! 25 Feb 2016 2:22

Early on Ted Cruz said that if he didn't win South Carolina it's over. He didn't win- and lost to me in a landslide! 25 Feb 2016 18:58

@tdltdltdltdl: Marco Cruz and Ted Rubio (easy to get the two politicians confused) looked like desperate panicked DC insiders tonight 26 Feb 2016 12:28

@donell27743094: @realDonaldTrump trump won the debate. Disgusting Rubio said peed" - is he still in junior high school." 26 Feb 2016 12:29

Have a good chance to win Texas on Tuesday. Cruz is a nasty guy not one Senate endorsement and despite talk gets nothing done. Loser! 26 Feb 2016 14:02

Why would the people of Florida vote for Marco Rubio when he defrauded them by agreeing to represent them as their Senator and then quit! 26 Feb 2016 14:49

Lying Ted Cruz and lightweight choker Marco Rubio teamed up last night in a last ditch effort to stop our great movement. They failed! 26 Feb 2016 16:15

Lightweight choker Marco Rubio looks like a little boy on stage. Not presidential material! 26 Feb 2016 16:16

Lightweight Marco Rubio was working hard last night. The problem is he is a choker and once a choker always a choker! Mr. Meltdown. 26 Feb 2016 16:38

They don't like Rubio in Florida- he left them high & dry. Doesn't even show up for votes! 26 Feb 2016 20:52

@donnieboysmith: @realDonaldTrump in contrast to Rubio and Cruz you look like a giant. They look terribly weak Thank you! 27 Feb 2016 3:08

@itsblakec: @realDonaldTrump Trump is a genius. Rubio and Cruz are not. I want a brilliant mind to run this country. 27 Feb 2016 4:53

@SassyPantsjj: Michigan GOP poll 2/24/2016 Trump 35.5 Rubio 15.0 Cruz 14.3 Kasich 12.8 Carson 8.3 @realDonaldTrump Wow! 27 Feb 2016 12:47

I will be on @foxandfriends at 8:30 A.M. Will be talking about lightweight Marco Rubio and lying Ted Cruz! 27 Feb 2016 13:08

I am self-funding my campaign and am therefore not controlled by the lobbyists and special interests like lightweight Rubio or Ted Cruz! 27 Feb 2016 15:25

I only wish my wonderful father Fred gave me $200 million to start my business like lightweight Rubio says. He didn't - total fabrication! 27 Feb 2016 16:04

Just watched lightweight Marco Rubio lying to a small crowd about my past record. He is not as smart as Cruz and may be an even bigger liar 27 Feb 2016 21:20

@sprivitor @realDonaldTrump Marco 'Amnesty' Rubio is the front man of Amnesty. #AlwaysTrump #Trump2016 #TrumpTrain 28 Feb 2016 10:54

@JimmyTheSaint09: @realDonaldTrump @RonnieMemo @ChrisChristie anything is better than @marcorubio 28 Feb 2016 10:56

@CharlesHodgson1: A lot more water after this bombshell Rubio. You are an enemy of America. @realDonaldTrump 28 Feb 2016 11:15

While I hear the Koch brothers are in big financial trouble (oil) word is they have chosen little Marco Rubio the lightweight from Florida 28 Feb 2016 11:28

The Republican Establishment has been pushing for lightweight Senator Marco Rubio to say anything to "hit" Trump.I signed the pledge-careful 28 Feb 2016 12:10

Little Marco Rubio the lightweight no show Senator from Florida is set to be the "puppet" of the special interest Koch brothers. WATCH! 28 Feb 2016 16:07

Why would the people of Texas support Ted Cruz when he has accomplished absolutely nothing for them. He is another all talk no action pol! 28 Feb 2016 16:47

Little Marco Rubio the lightweight no show Senator from

Florida is just another Washington politician. 28 Feb 2016 17:50

Lightweight Senator Marco Rubio is polling very poorly in Florida. The people can't stand him for missing so many votes - poor work ethic! 28 Feb 2016 17:53

@EmaGabi23: Rubio was kicking back on his $80k boat he bought with lobbyist money and claimed it was from book sale profit lol 28 Feb 2016 17:57

Little Marco Rubio is just another Washington D.C. politician that is all talk and no action. #RobotRubio 28 Feb 2016 18:45

Little Marco Rubio gave amnesty to criminal aliens guilty of "sex offenses." DISGRACE! 28 Feb 2016 19:06

Little Marco Rubio treated America's ICE officers "like absolute trash" in order to pass Obama's amnesty. 28 Feb 2016 19:19

Phylis Schlafly: 'Marco Rubio Betrayed Us All' 28 Feb 2016 19:32

Governor Alejandro García Padilla said presidential hopeful Sen. Marco Rubio "is no friend of Puerto Rico." 29 Feb 2016 16:29

Phony Rubio commercial. I could have settled but won't out of principle! See student surveys. 29 Feb 2016 22:59

RT @DanScavino: .@NikkiHaley in 2012 w/ Romney on tax returns??(political ploy.) Fast forward..2016 w/ Robot Rubio??#FAIL??#Politician 1 Mar 2016 19:14

RT @CLewandowski_: Gov Nikki Haley just became a liability for Rubio after this was published to social media! 1 Mar 2016 19:14

@mikiebarb: A nearly impossible path to the GOP nomination" for Rubio says @apalmerdc: 2 Mar 2016 12:22

@NorahODonnell: Looks like Rubio won't get any delegates from TX or AL because he didn't meet 20% threshold. 2 Mar 2016 12:23

@JoeNBC: Marco Rubio just criticized Ted Cruz for underperforming tonight. Wow. #SuperTuesday 2 Mar 2016 12:23

@JoeNBC: FOX calls Virginia for Trump. If it holds it's a big win for Trump and a big setback for Rubio who needed to win the state. 2 Mar 2016 12:25

Millions of dollars being spent on false TV ads by special interest groups who own Rubio & Cruz.When you see them think of your puppet POLS 3 Mar 2016 3:18

New ad concerning lightweight Senator Marco Rubio: 7 Mar 2016 23:48

Cruz came to Mississippi there was nobody there he left the state. I had a rally in Madison MS with 10000! Thank you! 8 Mar 2016 1:49

Ted Cruz Was For Welcoming Syrian Refugees Before He Was Against It 8 Mar 2016 2:47

Sun Sentinel says: Rubio lacks the experience work ethic and gravitas needed to be president. HE HAS NOT EARNED YOUR VOTE! 8 Mar 2016 16:12

Another Dishonest Politician #LightweightSenatorMarcoRubio 9 Mar 2016 23:00

Absentee Governor Kasich voted for NAFTA and NAFTA devastated Ohio - a disaster from which it never recovered. Kasich is good for Mexico! 12 Mar 2016 13:35

Ohio had the biggest budget increase in the U.S. If it were not for striking oil they would be bust! Governor Kasich in favor of TPP fraud! 12 Mar 2016 14:17

We are asking law enforcement to check for dishonest early voting in Florida- on behalf of little Marco Rubio. No way to run a country! 12 Mar 2016 18:07

Do the people of Ohio know that John Kasich is STRONGLY in favor of Common Core! In other words education of your children from D.C. No way 12 Mar 2016 22:47

Wow Kasich didn't qualify to run in the state of Pennsylvania not enough signatures. Big problem! 13 Mar 2016 3:30

Ohio Gov.Kasich voted for NAFTA from which Ohio has never recovered. Now he wants TPP which will be even worse. Ohio steel and coal dying! 13 Mar 2016 11:58

Gov.Kasich of Ohio just stated on a morning show that he

doesn't watch politics or anything on television he only watches the @GolfChannel 13 Mar 2016 14:49

Carly Fiorina- I agree! Ted Cruz is just another politician. All talk- no action! 13 Mar 2016 17:07

Because Gov. Kasich cannot run in the state of Pennsylvania-he cannot win the nomination- & should not be allowed to compete in Ohio on Tue. 13 Mar 2016 18:26

Gov Kasich voted for NAFTA which devastated Ohio and is now pushing TPP hard- bad for American workers! 14 Mar 2016 16:59

Kasich has helped decimate the coal and steel industries in Ohio. I will bring them back! #MakeAmericaGreatAgain 14 Mar 2016 16:59

Kasich voted for NAFTA a disaster for Ohio and now wants the even worse TPP approved. Vote Trump and end this madness! 15 Mar 2016 4:10

Rubio is weak on illegal immigration with the worst voting record in the U.S. Senate in many years. He will never MAKE AMERICA GREAT AGAIN! 15 Mar 2016 4:21

Please remember I am the ONLY candidate who is self-funding his campaign. Kasich Rubio and Cruz are all bought and paid for by lobbyists! 15 Mar 2016 10:39

Don't reward Mitt Romney who let us all down in the last presidential race by voting for Kasich (who voted for NAFTA open borders etc.). 15 Mar 2016 11:31

RT @EricTrump: Mathematically it is statistically impossible for Kasich to get to 1237 - he would need 112% of the remaining delegates to b... 15 Mar 2016 14:36

Watching John Kasich being interviewed - acting so innocent and like such a nice guy. Remember him in second debate until I put him down. 15 Mar 2016 14:53

Ohio is losing jobs to Mexico now losing Ford (and many others). Kasich is weak on illegal immigration. We need strong borders now! 15 Mar 2016 15:03

In presidential voting so far John Kasich is ZERO for 22. So why would he be a good candidate? Hillary would beat him I will beat Hillary! 15 Mar 2016 16:03

Yesterday was amazing—5 victories. Lyin' Ted Cruzhad zero. Things are going very well! 16 Mar 2016 17:04

Crazy @megynkelly supposedly had lyin' Ted Cruz on her show last night. Ted is desperate and his lying is getting worse. Ted can't win! 17 Mar 2016 10:17

Great news that @FoxNews has cancelled the additional debate. How many times can the same people ask the same question? I beat Cruz debating 17 Mar 2016 10:40

The reason lyin' Ted Cruz has lost so much of the evangelical vote is that they are very smart and just don't tolerate liars-a big problem! 17 Mar 2016 12:28

Who should star in a reboot of Liar Liar- Hillary Clinton or Ted Cruz? Let me know. 17 Mar 2016 18:33

Lyin' Ted Cruz lost all five races on Tuesday-and he was just given the jinx - a Lindsey Graham endorsement. Also backed Jeb. Lindsey got 0! 18 Mar 2016 16:42

Senator @LindseyGrahamSC made horrible statements about @SenTedCruz – and then he endorsed him. No wonder nobody trusts politicians! 18 Mar 2016 19:03

Going to Salt Lake City Utah for a big rally. Lyin' Ted Cruz should not be allowed to win there - Mormons don't like LIARS! I beat Hillary 18 Mar 2016 20:07

Failed presidential candidate Mitt Romney the man who "choked" and let us all down is now endorsing Lyin' Ted Cruz. This is good for me! 18 Mar 2016 20:18

Failed Presidential Candidate Mitt Romney was campaigning with John Kasich & Marco Rubio and now he is endorsing Ted Cruz. 1/2 18 Mar 2016 20:21

Why haven't they released the final Missouri victory for us yet? Could it be because Cruz's guy runs Missouri? 19 Mar 2016 1:53

Lyin' Ted Cruz just used a picture of Melania from a G.Q. shoot in his ad. Be careful Lyin' Ted or I will spill the beans on your wife! 23 Mar 2016 1:53

Lyin' Ted Cruz denied that he had anything to do with the G.Q. model photo post of Melania. That's why we call him Lyin' Ted! 23 Mar 2016 14:22

Lyin' Ted Cruz steals foreign policy from me and lines from Michael Douglas— just another dishonest politician. 23 Mar 2016 19:45

Low energy Jeb Bush just endorsed a man he truly hates Lyin' Ted Cruz. Honestly I can't blame Jeb in that I drove him into oblivion! 23 Mar 2016 19:49

I think having Jeb's endorsement hurts Lyin' Ted. Jeb spent more than $150000000 and got nothing. I spent a fraction of that and am first! 23 Mar 2016 20:02

.@LindseyGrahamSC and Lyin' Ted Cruz are two politicians who are very much alike - ALL TALK AND NO ACTION! Both talk about ISIS do nothing! 24 Mar 2016 14:07

These politicians like Cruz and Graham who have watched ISIS and many other problems develop for years do nothing to make things better! 24 Mar 2016 14:14

@NeilTurner_: @realDonaldTrump Cruz & Rubio are scared! WATCH 24 Mar 2016 15:59

Endorsements for Lyin' Ted Cruz- 24 Mar 2016 16:02

I didn't start the fight with Lyin'Ted Cruz over the GQ cover pic of Melania he did. He knew the PAC was putting it out - hence Lyin' Ted! 24 Mar 2016 22:31

Lyin' Ted Cruz is now trying to convince prople that his problems with The National Enq.were caused by me. I had NOTHING to do with story! 26 Mar 2016 19:13

Just to show you how unfair Republican primary politics can be I won the State of Louisiana and get less delegates than Cruz-Lawsuit coming 27 Mar 2016 21:11

See Lyin' Ted even the @DailyBeast (no fan of mine) says this story came from Rubio not Trump! 27 Mar 2016 22:16

Kirsten Powers: Anti- Trump Operative was Aggressively Shopping Cruz Story via the Gateway Pundit: 28 Mar 2016 14:45

Ted Cruz is incensed that I want to refocus NATO on terrorism as well as current mission but also want others to PAY FAIR SHARE a must! 28 Mar 2016 22:18

@wolfblitzer: Campaign-to-date popular GOP totals: @realDonaldTrump 7546980; @tedcruz 5481737; @JohnKasich 2724749 A BIG DIFFERENCE 28 Mar 2016 22:22

After the way I beat Gov. Scott Walker (and Jeb Rand Marco and all others) in the Presidential Primaries no way he would ever endorse me! 28 Mar 2016 23:13

Lyin'Ted Cruz is weak & losing big so now he wants to debate again. But according to DrudgeTime and on-line polls I have won all debates 29 Mar 2016 0:57

I have millions more votes/hundreds more dels than Cruz or Kasich and yet am not being treated properly by the Republican Party or the RNC. 29 Mar 2016 14:16

How come the @TODAYshow & @chucktodd show the new @NBCNews Poll for Hillary vs Bernie but do not show the SAME poll where I am killing Cruz? 29 Mar 2016 14:45

The Club For Growth said in their ad that 465 delegates (Cruz) plus 143 delegates (Kasich) is more than my 739 delegates. Try again! 1 Apr 2016 4:29

Can you believe that Ted Cruz who has been killing our country on trade for so long just put out a Wisconsin ad talking about trade? 1 Apr 2016 21:52

Ted Cruz attacked New Yorkers and New York values- we don't forget! 7 Apr 2016 19:31

I win a state in votes and then get non-representative delegates because they are offered all sorts of goodies by Cruz campaign. Bad system! 10 Apr 2016 13:47

Lyin' Ted Cruz will never be able to beat Hillary. Despite a rigged delegate system I am hundreds of delegates ahead of him. 17 Apr 2016 13:34

Lyin' Ted Cruz can't get votes (I am millions ahead of him) so he has to get his delegates from the Republican bosses. It won't work! 17 Apr 2016 13:38

Lyin' Ted Cruz can't win with the voters so he has to sell himself to the bosses-I am millions of VOTES ahead! Hillary would destroy him & K 18 Apr 2016 10:58

Kasich only looks O.K. in polls against Hillary because nobody views him as a threat and therefore have placed ZERO negative ads against him 18 Apr 2016 11:02

Lyin' Ted Cruz even voted against Superstorm Sandy aid and September 11th help. So many New Yorkers devastated. Cruz hates New York! 18 Apr 2016 21:54

Ted Cruz is mathematically out of winning the race. Now all he can do is be a spoiler never a nice thing to do. I will beat Hillary! 20 Apr 2016 12:42

Senator Ted Cruz has been MATHEMATICALLY ELIMINATED from race. He said Kasich should get out for same reason. I think both should get out! 21 Apr 2016 10:22

Both Ted Cruz and John Kasich have no path to victory. They should both drop out of the race so that the Republican Party can unify! 21 Apr 2016 21:47

Cruz said Kasich should leave because he couldn't get to 1237. Now he can't get to 1237. Drop out LYIN' Ted. 21 Apr 2016 22:16

As soon as John Kasich is hit with negative ads he will drop like a rock in the polls against Crooked Hillary Clinton. I will win! 24 Apr 2016 1:48

Wow just announced that Lyin' Ted and Kasich are going to collude in order to keep me from getting the Republican nomination. DESPERATION! 25 Apr 2016 3:39

Lyin' Ted and Kasich are mathematically dead and totally desperate. Their donors & special interest groups are not happy with them. Sad! 25 Apr 2016 3:49

Lyin' Ted Cruz and 1 for 38 Kasich are unable to beat me on their own so they have to team up (collusion) in a two on one. Shows weakness! 25 Apr 2016 11:54

Kasich just announced that he wants the people of Indiana to vote for him. Typical politician - can't make a deal work. 25 Apr 2016 16:15

The Cruz-Kasich pact is under great strain. This joke of a deal is falling apart not being honored and almost dead. Very dumb! 26 Apr 2016 10:42

Lyin' Ted Cruz who can never beat Hillary Clinton and has NO path to victory has chosen a V.P.candidate who failed badly in her own effort 28 Apr 2016 11:31

RT @AdrianaCohen16: Carly Fiorina no lifeboat for a fast-sinking @tedcruz campaign via @bostonherald @realdonaldtru... 29 Apr 2016 0:32

Wow the ridiculous deal made between Lyin'Ted Cruz and 1 for 42 John Kasich has just blown up. What a dumb deal - dead on arrival! 29 Apr 2016 11:22

.@KarlRove is a failed Jeb Bushy. Never says anything good & never will even after I beat Hillary. Shouldn't be on the air! 1 May 2016 20:06

Wow Lyin' Ted Cruz really went wacko today. Made all sorts of crazy charges. Can't function under pressure - not very presidential. Sad! 3 May 2016 23:02

Lyin' Ted Cruz consistently said that he will and must win Indiana. If he doesn't he should drop out of the race-stop wasting time & money 3 May 2016 23:08

Joe Scarborough initially endorsed Jeb Bush and Jeb crashed then John Kasich and that didn't work. Not much power or insight! 6 May 2016 18:03

Remember when the two failed presidential candidates Lindsey Graham and Jeb Bush signed a binding PLEDGE? They broke the deal no honor! 7 May 2016 17:46

The @washingtonpost report on potential VP candidates is wrong. Marco Rubio and most others mentioned are NOT under consideration. 16 May 2016 1:25

Poll data shows that @marcorubio does by far the best in holding onto his Senate seat in Florida. Important to keep the MAJORITY. Run Marco! 27 May 2016 2:09

@mabynshingleton: JohnKasich the VOTERS have spoken.We want @realDonaldTrump. You AGREED to support NOMINEE. Get on board or leave @GOP 9 Jun 2016 1:00

John Kasich was never asked by me to be V.P. Just arrived in Cleveland - will be a great two days! 20 Jul 2016 18:48

Wow Ted Cruz got booed off the stage didn't honor the pledge! I saw his speech two hours early but let him speak anyway. No big deal! 21 Jul 2016 3:45

Ted Cruz talks about the Constitution but doesn't say that if the Dems win the Presidency the new JUSTICES appointed will destroy us all! 21 Jul 2016 14:12

Our not very bright Vice President Joe Biden just stated that I wanted to "carpet bomb" the enemy. Sorry Joe that was Ted Cruz! 27 Jul 2016 12:57

The @SenTedCruz endorsement was a wonderful surprise. I greatly appreciate his support! We will have a tremendous victory on November 8th. 24 Sep 2016 12:35

Thank you Senator @TedCruz!#Debates2016 #MAGA 27 Sep 2016 3:58

Jeb Bush George W and George H.W. all called to express their best wishes on the win. Very nice! 13 Nov 2016 15:23

Governor John Kasich of the GREAT GREAT GREAT State of Ohio called to congratulate me on the win. The people of Ohio were incredible! 13 Nov 2016 15:28

Crooked Hillary

Crooked Hillary Clinton is spending a fortune on ads against me. I am the one person she doesn't want to run against. Will be such fun! 17 Apr 2016 13:41

Crooked Hillary Clinton perhaps the most dishonest person to have ever run for the presidency is also one of the all time great enablers! 29 Apr 2016 13:46

Crooked Hillary Clinton said she is used to "dealing with men who get off the reservation." Actually she has done poorly with such men! 2 May 2016 11:12

I will defeat Crooked Hillary Clinton on 11/8/2016. #Trump2016#MakeAmericaGreatAgain 2 May 2016 16:16

What a great evening we had. So interesting that Sanders beat Crooked Hillary. The dysfunctional system is totally rigged against him! 4 May 2016 9:25

I would rather run against Crooked Hillary Clinton than Bernie Sanders and that will happen because the books are cooked against Bernie! 4 May 2016 9:44

Can you believe Crooked Hillary said "We are going to put a whole lot of coal miners&coal companies out of business." She then apologized. 6 May 2016 1:57

Unlike crooked Hillary Clinton who wants to destroy all miners I want wages to go up in America. We will do so by bringing back jobs! 6 May 2016 10:14

Crooked Hillary has ZERO leadership ability. As Bernie Sanders says she has bad judgement. Constantly playing the women's card - it is sad! 6 May 2016 12:38

I hear @JoeNBC of rapidly fading @Morning_Joe is pushing hard for a third party candidate to run. This will guarantee a Crooked Hillary win. 6 May 2016 18:25

Crooked Hillary Clinton wants completely open borders. Millions of Democrats will run from her over this and support me. 7 May 2016 0:16

I am going to keep our jobs in the U.S. and totally rebuild our crumbling infrastructure. Crooked Hillary has no clue! @Teamsters 7 May 2016 15:47

Crooked Hillary just can't close the deal with Bernie. It will be the same way with ISIS and China on trade and Mexico at the border. Bad! 8 May 2016 20:15

I will win the election against Crooked Hillary despite the people in the Republican Party that are currently and selfishly opposed to me! 9 May 2016 9:32

Crooked Hillary Clinton says that she got more primary votes than Donald Trump. But I had 17 people to beat—she had one! 9 May 2016 16:56

Why does the media with a strong push from Crooked Hillary keep pushing the false narrative that I want to raise taxes. Exactly opposite! 10 May 2016 12:57

It was Rosie O'Donnell who ate the cake in the vicious Hillary commercial about me not Crooked Hillary! @marthamaccallum 10 May 2016 13:57

The Clintons spend millions on negative ads on me & I can't tell the truth about her husband? Don't feel sorry for crooked Hillary! 10 May 2016 19:31

Big wins in West Virginia and Nebraska. Get ready for November - Crooked Hillary who is looking very bad against Crazy Bernie will lose! 11 May 2016 10:22

I don't want to hit Crazy Bernie Sanders too hard yet because I love watching what he is doing to Crooked Hillary. His time will come! 11 May 2016 10:26

Goofy Elizabeth Warren is now using the woman's card like her friend crooked Hillary. See her dumb tweet "when a woman stands up to you..." 11 May 2016 19:37

If Crooked Hillary Clinton can't close the deal on Crazy Bernie how is she going to take on China Russia ISIS and all of the others? 14 May 2016 1:03

Wow 30000 e-mails were deleted by Crooked Hillary Clinton. She said they had to do with a wedding reception. Liar! How can she run? 17 May 2016 11:29

Crooked Hillary Clinton put out an ad where I am misquoted on women. Can't believe she would misrepresent the facts! My hit was on China 17 May 2016 11:46

Amazing that Crooked Hillary can do a hit ad on me concerning women when her husband was the WORST abuser of woman in U.S. political history 17 May 2016 11:58

Crooked Hillary can't close the deal with Bernie Sanders. Will be another bad day for her! 17 May 2016 12:31

Crooked Hillary said her husband is going to be in charge of the economy.If so he should runnot her.Will he bring the "energizer" to D.C.? 17 May 2016 14:17

How can Crooked Hillary put her husband in charge of the economy when he was responsible for NAFTA the worst economic deal in U.S. history? 17 May 2016 14:21

Do you think Crooked Hillary will finally close the deal? If she can't win Kentucky she should drop out of race. System rigged! 17 May 2016 23:37

Wall Street paid for ad is a fraud just like Crooked Hillary! Their main line had nothing to do with women and they knew it. Apologize? 17 May 2016 23:42

I look so forward to debating Crooked Hillary Clinton! Democrat Primaries are rigged e-mail investigation is rigged - so time to get it on! 18 May 2016 1:53

Why did Clinton supporter @AlisonForKY declare Crooked Hillary winner in KY when AP hasn't even called the race? 18 May 2016 16:39

I said that Crooked Hillary Clinton is "not qualified" to be president because she has "very bad judgement" - Bernie said the same thing! 20 May 2016 9:40

Crooked Hillary has zero imagination and even less stamina. ISIS China Russia and all would love for her to be president. 4 more years! 20 May 2016 9:47

Crooked Hillary Clinton looks presidential? I don't think so! Four more years of Obama and our country will never come back. ISIS LAUGHS! 20 May 2016 10:08

Crooked Hillary can't even close the deal with Bernie - and the Dems have it rigged in favor of Hillary. Four more years of this? No way! 20 May 2016 10:26

Crooked Hillary Clinton- discussing the #SecondAmendment at a private event. #2A cc: @NRA 20 May 2016 15:36

Crooked Hillary Clinton wants to essentially abolish the 2nd Amendment. No gun owner can ever vote for Clinton! 21 May 2016 1:51

Crooked Hillary is spending tremendous amounts of Wall Street money on false ads against me. She is a very dishonest person! 21 May 2016 1:56

Crooked Hillary wants to get rid of all guns and yet she is surrounded by bodyguards who are fully armed. No more guns to protect Hillary! 21 May 2016 12:49

Crooked Hillary Clintons foreign interventions unleashed ISIS in Syria Iraq and Libya. She is reckless and dangerous! 21 May 2016 17:02

Crooked Hillary said that I want guns brought into the school classroom. Wrong! 22 May 2016 3:55

RT @gatewaypundit: BREAKING POLL: Trump Gains 11 Points on Clinton Since March=> Now Leads Crooked Hillary 46-44 22 May 2016 15:28

How can Crooked Hillary say she cares about women when she is silent on radical Islam which horribly oppresses women? 22 May 2016 19:37

Crooked Hillary wants a radical 500% increase in Syrian refugees. We can't allow this. Time to get smart and protect America! 22 May 2016 19:38

Bernie Sanders is continuing his quest because he believes that Crooked Hillary Clinton will be forced out of the race - e-mail scandal! 22 May 2016 20:32

Crooked Hillary Clinton overregulates overtaxes and doesn't care about jobs. Most importantly she suffers from plain old bad judgement! 24 May 2016 11:42

A great new book has been written about Crooked Hillary. Read it & you will never be able to vote for her. @Ed_Klein 24 May 2016 14:35

After raising w/ no obligation almost $6M for Vets I couldn't believe protesters formed @ Trump Tower. JUST OUT- SENT BY CROOKED HILLARY! 25 May 2016 0:32

Crooked Hillary Clinton just can't close the deal with Bernie. I had to knock out 16 very good and smart candidates. Hillary doesn't have it 25 May 2016 13:14

The Inspector General's report on Crooked Hillary Clinton is a disaster. Such bad judgement and temperament cannot be allowed in the W.H. 26 May 2016 13:18

I would have had millions of votes more in the primaries (than Crooked Hillary) if I only had one opponent instead of sixteen. Broke record 30 May 2016 20:13

I am getting great credit for my press conference today. Crooked Hillary should be admonished for not having a press conference in 179 days. 31 May 2016 23:17

Crooked Hillary Clinton is a fraud who has put the public and country at risk by her illegal and very stupid use of e-mails. Many missing! 1 Jun 2016 22:16

Crooked Hillary Clinton has zero natural talent - she should not be president. Her temperament is bad and her decision making ability-zilch! 2 Jun 2016 15:03

Bernie Sanders was right when he said that Crooked Hillary Clinton was not qualified to be president because she suffers from BAD judgement! 2 Jun 2016 15:10

With all of the Crooked Hillary Clinton's foreign policy experience she has made so many mistakes - and I mean real monsters! No more HRC. 2 Jun 2016 16:48

Crooked Hillary Clinton who I would love to call Lyin' Hillary is getting ready to totally misrepresent my foreign policy positions. 2 Jun 2016 17:06

Crooked Hillary no longer has credibility - too much failure in office. People will not allow another four years of incompetence! 2 Jun 2016 19:15

Bad performance by Crooked Hillary Clinton! Reading poorly from the telepromter! She doesn't even look presidential! 2 Jun 2016 19:18

In Crooked Hillary's telepromter speech yesterday she made up things that I said or believe but have no basis in fact. Not honest! 3 Jun 2016 13:13

Crooked Hillary Clinton has not held a news conference in more than 7 months. Her record is so bad she is unable to answer tough questions! 6 Jun 2016 13:15

Crooked Hillary is being badly criticized (for a Wall Street paid for ad) by PolitiFact for a false ad on me on women. She is a total fraud! 6 Jun 2016 13:23

A former Secret Service Agent for President Clinton excoriates Crooked Hillary describing her as ERRATIC & VIOLENT. Bad temperament for pres 7 Jun 2016 1:51

In just out book Secret Service Agent Gary Byrne doesn't believe that Crooked Hillary has the temperament or integrity to be the president! 7 Jun 2016 2:21

I would have had many millions of votes more than Crooked Hillary Clinton except for the fact that I had 16 opponents she had one! 9 Jun 2016 0:54

Bernie Sanders must really dislike Crooked Hillary after the way she played him. Many of his supporters because of trade will come to me. 9 Jun 2016 1:46

Crooked Hillary Clinton will be a disaster on jobs the economy trade healthcare the military guns and just about all else. Obama plus! 9 Jun 2016 12:29

Obama just endorsed Crooked Hillary. He wants four more years of Obama—but nobody else does! 9 Jun 2016 18:22

2004 VIDEO:Pocahontas describing Crooked Hillary Clinton as a Corporate Donor Puppet. Time for change! #Trump2016 10 Jun 2016 16:12

I rarely agree with President Obama- however he is 100% correct about Crooked Hillary Clinton. Great ad! 10 Jun 2016 16:49

I have been hitting Obama and Crooked Hillary hard on not using the term Radical Islamic Terror. Hillary just broke-said she would now use! 13 Jun 2016 14:59

Crooked Hillary says we must call on Saudi Arabia and other countries to stop funding hate. I am calling on- cont'd: 13 Jun 2016 21:35

People very unhappy with Crooked Hillary and Obama on JOBS and SAFETY! Biggest trade deficit in many years! More attacks will follow Orlando 17 Jun 2016 11:20

Crooked Hillary Clinton is totally unfit to be our president-really bad judgement and a temperament according to new book which is a mess! 21 Jun 2016 10:38

I will be making a big speech tomorrow to discuss the failed policies and bad judgment of Crooked Hillary Clinton. 21 Jun 2016 14:22

Crooked Hillary refuses to say that she will be raising taxes beyond belief! She will be a disaster for jobs and the economy! 22 Jun 2016 3:16

Crooked Hillary called it totally wrong on BREXIT - she went with Obama - and now she is saying we need her to lead. She would be a disaster 24 Jun 2016 21:23

So funny Crooked Hillary called BREXIT so incorrectly and now she says that she is the one to deal with the U.K. All talk no action! 25 Jun 2016 12:00

Crooked Hillary Clinton who called BREXIT 100% wrong (along with Obama) is now spending Wall Street money on an ad on my correct call. 26 Jun 2016 11:33

Crooked Hillary just took a major ad of me playing golf at Turnberry. Shows me hitting shot but I never did = lie! Was there to support son 26 Jun 2016 16:06

Top 50 Facts About Crooked Hillary Clinton From Trump 'Stakes Of The Election' Address: 26 Jun 2016 16:31

People in our country want borders and without them the old line pols like Crooked Hillary will not win. It is time for CHANGE -- and JOBS! 26 Jun 2016 21:21

Crooked Hillary Clinton got Brexit wrong. I said LEAVE will win. She has no sense of markets and such bad judgement. Only a question of time 26 Jun 2016 22:15

Crooked Hillary Attacks Foreign Government Donations - While Ignoring Her Own: 26 Jun 2016 22:28

Crooked Hillary is wheeling out one of the least productive senators in the U.S. Senate goofy Elizabeth Warren who lied on heritage. 27 Jun 2016 13:07

Check it out - 2nd video on Lying Crooked Hillary is now online! Watch it here: #CrookedHillary #Trump2016 28 Jun 2016 19:30

Why would college graduates want Crooked Hillary as their President? She will destroy them! 30 Jun 2016 18:53

Crooked Hillary -- Makes History! #ImWithYou #AmericaFirst 2 Jul 2016 15:19

It was just announced-by sources-that no charges will be brought against Crooked Hillary Clinton. Like I said the system is totally rigged! 2 Jul 2016 21:13

Only a fool would believe that the meeting between Bill Clinton and the U.S.A.G. was not arranged or that Crooked Hillary did not know. 3 Jul 2016 20:16

Crooked Hillary Clinton knew that her husband wanted to meet with the U.S.A.G. to work out a deal. The system is totally rigged & corrupt! 3 Jul 2016 20:20

I believe that Crooked Hillary sent Bill to have the meeting with the U.S.A.G. So Bill is not in trouble with H except that he got caught! 3 Jul 2016 21:46

Crooked Hillary will NEVER be able to handle the complexities and danger of ISIS - it will just go on forever. We need change! 4 Jul 2016 12:00

Crooked Hillary Clinton is "guilty as hell" but the system is totally rigged and corrupt! Where are the 33000 missing e-mails? 4 Jul 2016 15:26

Why is President Obama allowed to use Air Force One on the campaign trail with Crooked Hillary? She is flying with him tomorrow. Who pays? 4 Jul 2016 22:30

Taxpayers are paying a fortune for the use of Air Force One on the campaign trail by President Obama and Crooked Hillary. A total disgrace! 5 Jul 2016 11:14

FBI director said Crooked Hillary compromised our national security. No charges. Wow! #RiggedSystem 5 Jul 2016 15:39

I don't think the voters will forget the rigged system that allowed Crooked Hillary to get away with "murder." Come November 8 she's out! 6 Jul 2016 4:30

Crooked Hillary Clinton is unfit to serve as President of the U.S. Her temperament is weak and her opponents are strong. BAD JUDGEMENT! 6 Jul 2016 4:36

Crooked Hillary Clinton and her team "were extremely careless in their handling of very sensitive highly classified information." Not fit! 6 Jul 2016 11:12

Crooked Hillary has once again been proven to be a person who is dishonest incompetent and of very bad judgement. 6 Jul 2016 11:21

Crooked Hillary Clinton lied to the FBI and to the people of our country. She is sooooo guilty. But watch her time will come! 6 Jul 2016 12:31

I have over seven million hits on social media re Crooked Hillary Clinton. Check it out Sleepy Eyes @MarkHalperin @NBCPolitics 6 Jul 2016 14:06

Convention speaker schedule to be released tomorrow. Let today be devoted to Crooked Hillary and the rigged system under which we live. 6 Jul 2016 15:32

To all of my twitter followers please contribute whatever you can to the campaign. We must beat Crooked Hillary. 6 Jul 2016 21:58

After today Crooked Hillary can officially be called Lyin' Crooked Hillary. 8 Jul 2016 1:52

Look what is happening to our country under the WEAK leadership of Obama and people like Crooked Hillary Clinton. We are a divided nation! 10 Jul 2016 12:02

Bernie Sanders who has lost most of his leverage has totally sold out to Crooked Hillary Clinton. He will endorse her today - fans angry! 12 Jul 2016 13:36

Bernie Sanders endorsing Crooked Hillary Clinton is like Occupy Wall Street endorsing Goldman Sachs. 12 Jul 2016 17:01

Bernie sanders has abandoned his supporters by endorsing pro-war pro-TPP pro-Wall Street Crooked Hillary Clinton. 12 Jul 2016 17:03

Lyin' Crooked Hillary's email stories all have one thing in common. 13 Jul 2016 22:11

Voters understand that Crooked Hillary's negative ads are not true- just like her email lies and her other fraudulent activity. 13 Jul 2016 22:22

I employ many people in the State of Virginia - JOBS JOBS JOBS! Crooked Hillary will sell us out just like her husband did with NAFTA. 14 Jul 2016 17:23

Four more years of weakness with a Crooked Hillary Administration is not acceptable. Look what has happened to the world with O & Hillary! 15 Jul 2016 14:41

Crooked Hillary is spending big Wall Street money on ads saying I don't have foreign policy experience yet look what her policies have done 16 Jul 2016 13:08

Crooked Hillary who embarrassed herself and the country with her e-mail lies has been a DISASTER on foreign policy. Look what's happening! 16 Jul 2016 13:13

Very sad that a person who has made so many mistakes Crooked Hillary Clinton can put out such false and vicious ads with her phony money! 16 Jul 2016 13:19

Crooked Hillary Clinton is bought and paid for by Wall Street lobbyists and special interests. She will sell our country down the tubes! 16 Jul 2016 13:23

Donate Today To Help Make America Great Again! You Can Help Stop Crooked Hillary Clinton! 16 Jul 2016 20:44

Donate Today To Help Make America Great Again! You Can Help Stop Crooked Hillary Clinton! 16 Jul 2016 21:01

As the days and weeks go by we see what a total mess our country (and world) is in - Crooked Hillary Clinton led Obama into bad decisions! 17 Jul 2016 11:55

It doesn't matter that Crooked Hillary has experience look at all of the bad decisions she has made. Bernie said she has bad judgement! 17 Jul 2016 12:06

I hope that Crooked Hillary picks Goofy Elizabeth Warren sometimes referred to as Pocahontas as her V.P. Then we can litigate her fraud! 17 Jul 2016 12:14

.@FoxNews is much better and far more truthful than @CNN which is all negative. Guests are stacked for Crooked Hillary! I don't watch. 17 Jul 2016 13:04

Pocahontas wanted V.P. slot so badly but wasn't chosen because she has done nothing in the Senate. Also Crooked Hillary hates her! 23 Jul 2016 10:42

Crooked Hillary Clinton has destroyed jobs and manufacturing in Pennsylvania. Against steelworkers and miners. Husband signed NAFTA. 23 Jul 2016 14:51

Just saw Crooked Hillary and Tim Kaine together. ISIS and our other enemies are drooling. They don't look presidential to me! 23 Jul 2016 20:43

The Crooked Hillary V.P. choice is VERY disrespectful to Bernie Sanders and all of his supporters. Just another case of BAD JUDGEMENT by H! 24 Jul 2016 11:16

Crooked Hillary Clinton was not at all loyal to the person in her rigged system that pushed her over the top DWS. Too bad Bernie flamed out 24 Jul 2016 22:02

Even though Bernie Sanders has lost his energy and his strength I don't believe that his supporters will let Crooked Hillary off the hook! 24 Jul 2016 22:07

The highly neurotic Debbie Wasserman Schultz is angry that after stealing and cheating her way to a Crooked Hillary victory she's out! 24 Jul 2016 22:33

Watched Crooked Hillary Clinton and Tim Kaine on 60 Minutes. No way they are going to fix America's problems. ISIS & all others laughing! 24 Jul 2016 23:59

Crooked Hillary Clinton knew everything that her "servant" was doing at the DNC - they just got caught that's all! They laughed at Bernie. 25 Jul 2016 13:19

Here we go again with another Clinton scandal and e-mails yet (can you believe). Crooked Hillary knew the fix was in B never had a chance! 25 Jul 2016 13:42

The State of Florida is so embarrassed by the antics of Crooked Hillary Clinton and Debbie Wasserman Schultz that they will vote for CHANGE! 25 Jul 2016 14:01

Great POLL numbers are coming out all over. People don't want another four years of Obama and Crooked Hillary would be even worse. #MAGA 25 Jul 2016 14:05

Elizabeth Warren often referred to as Pocahontas just misrepresented me and spoke glowingly about Crooked Hillary who she always hated! 26 Jul 2016 3:12

Bernie Sanders totally sold out to Crooked Hillary Clinton. All of that work energy and money and nothing to show for it! Waste of time. 26 Jul 2016 3:19

The invention of email has proven to be a very bad thing for Crooked Hillary in that it has proven her to be both incompetent and a liar! 26 Jul 2016 19:27

Just like I have warned from the beginning Crooked Hillary Clinton will betray you on the TPP. 27 Jul 2016 3:01

As I have been saying Crooked Hillary will approve the job killing TPP after the election despite her statements to the contrary: top adv. 27 Jul 2016 9:33

Crooked Hillary Clinton wants to flood our country with Syrian immigrants that we know little or nothing about. The danger is massive. NO! 27 Jul 2016 10:08

Crooked Hillary Clinton made up facts about me and "forgot" to mention the many problems of our country in her very average scream! 29 Jul 2016 12:51

Crooked Hillary Clinton mentioned me 22 times in her very long and very boring speech. Many of her statements were lies and fabrications! 29 Jul 2016 13:44

Crooked Hillary said that I "couldn't handle the rough and tumble of a political campaign." ReallyI just beat 16 people and am beating her! 29 Jul 2016 14:14

Wow my campaign is hearing from more and more Bernie supporters that they will NEVER support Crooked Hillary. She sold them out V.P. pick! 29 Jul 2016 17:03

I am watching Crooked Hillary speak. Same old stuff our country needs change! 29 Jul 2016 17:43

What Bernie Sanders really thinks of Crooked Hillary Clinton. 29 Jul 2016 17:53

We are suffering through the worst long-term unemployment in the last 70 years. I want change - Crooked Hillary Clinton does not. 30 Jul 2016 12:57

Crooked Hillary Clinton is soft on crime supports open borders and wants massive tax hikes. A formula for disaster! 30 Jul 2016 18:07

Why doesn't the media want to report that on the two "Big Thursdays" when Crooked Hillary and I made our speeches - Republican's won ratings 30 Jul 2016 19:55

Word is that Crooked Hillary has very small and unenthusiastic crowds in Pennsylvania. Perhaps it is because her husband signed NAFTA? 30 Jul 2016 21:51

Thank you to all of the television viewers that made my speech at the Republican National Convention #1 over Crooked Hillary and DEMS. 30 Jul 2016 23:00

Crooked Hillary Clinton is 100% owned by her donors. #ImWithYou #MAGA 1 Aug 2016 21:42

Crooked Hillary said loudly and for the world to see that she "SHORT CIRCUITED" when answering a question on her e-mails. Very dangerous! 6 Aug 2016 14:24

I am not just running against Crooked Hillary Clinton I am running against the very dishonest and totally biased media - but I will win! 7 Aug 2016 1:53

A massive tax increase will be necessary to fund Crooked Hillary Clinton's agenda. What a terrible (and boring) rollout that was yesterday! 12 Aug 2016 11:07

Crooked Hillary Clinton is being protected by the media. She is not a talented person or politician. The dishonest media refuses to expose! 14 Aug 2016 16:50

I am not only fighting Crooked Hillary I am fighting the dishonest and corrupt media and her government protection process. People get it! 14 Aug 2016 16:55

Crooked Hillary is flooding the airwaves with false and misleading ads - all paid for by her bosses on Wall Street. Media is protecting her! 22 Aug 2016 0:33

Crooked Hillary will NEVER be able to solve the problems of poverty education and safety within the African-American & Hispanic communities 26 Aug 2016 13:50

How quickly people forget that Crooked Hillary called African-American youth "SUPER PREDATORS" - Has she apologized? 26 Aug 2016 17:14

I think that both candidates Crooked Hillary and myself should release detailed medical records. I have no problem in doing so! Hillary? 28 Aug 2016 23:24

Does anyone know that Crooked Hillary who tried so hard was unable to pass the Bar Exams in Washington D.C. She was forced to go elsewhere 29 Aug 2016 13:23

Crooked Hillary's brainpower is highly overrated.Probably why her decision making is so bad or as stated by Bernie S she has BAD JUDGEMENT 29 Aug 2016 13:30

.@CNN is so disgusting in their bias but they are having a hard time promoting Crooked Hillary in light of the new e-mail scandals. 3 Sep 2016 20:36

Crooked Hillary's V.P. pick said this morning that I was not aware that Russia took over Crimea. A total lie - and taken over during O term! 4 Sep 2016 16:04

The polls are close so Crooked Hillary is getting out of bed and will campaign tomorrow.Why did she hammer 13 devices and acid-wash e-mails? 4 Sep 2016 23:17

Crooked Hillary wants to take your 2nd Amendment rights away. Will guns be taken from her heavily armed Secret Service detail? Maybe not! 17 Sep 2016 5:53

The failing @nytimes has gone nuts that Crooked Hillary is doing so badly. They are willing to say anything has become a laughingstock rag! 17 Sep 2016 21:38

Crooked Hillary has been fighting ISIS or whatever she has been doing for years. Now she has new ideas. It is time for change. 20 Sep 2016 12:02

Crooked Hillary's bad judgement forced her to announce that she would go to Charlotte on Saturday to grandstand. Dem pols said no way dumb! 24 Sep 2016 2:09

I really enjoyed the debate last night.Crooked Hillary says she is going to do so many things.Why hasn't she done them in her last 30 years? 27 Sep 2016 12:53

Wow Crooked Hillary was duped and used by my worst Miss U. Hillary floated her as an "angel" without checking her past which is terrible! 30 Sep 2016 9:14

Using Alicia M in the debate as a paragon of virtue just shows that Crooked Hillary suffers from BAD JUDGEMENT! Hillary was set up by a con. 30 Sep 2016 9:19

Did Crooked Hillary help disgusting (check out sex tape and past) Alicia M become a U.S. citizen so she could use her in the debate? 30 Sep 2016 9:30

Wow just saw the really bad @CNN ratings. People don't want to watch bad product that only builds up Crooked Hillary. 1 Oct 2016 21:25

Bernie should pull his endorsement of Crooked Hillary after she decieved him and then attacked him and his supporters. 2 Oct 2016 21:48

Wow @CNN got caught fixing their "focus group" in order to make Crooked Hillary look better. Really pathetic and totally dishonest! 10 Oct 2016 19:31

Disloyal R's are far more difficult than Crooked Hillary. They come at you from all sides. They don't know how to win - I will teach them! 11 Oct 2016 14:48

Wow @CNN Town Hall questions were given to Crooked Hillary Clinton in advance of big debates against Bernie Sanders. Hillary & CNN FRAUD! 11 Oct 2016 23:04

Crooked Hillary Clinton likes to talk about the things she will do but she has been there for 30 years - why didn't she do them? 12 Oct 2016 12:59

This election is being rigged by the media pushing false and unsubstantiated charges and outright lies in order to elect Crooked Hillary! 15 Oct 2016 11:45

A country that Crooked Hillary says has funded ISIS also gave Wild Bill $1 million for his birthday? SO CORRUPT! 16 Oct 2016 13:15

The election is absolutely being rigged by the dishonest and distorted media pushing Crooked Hillary - but also at many polling places - SAD 16 Oct 2016 17:01

The Democrats have a corrupt political machine pushing crooked Hillary Clinton. We have Paul Ryan always fighting the Republican nominee! 16 Oct 2016 20:47

Wow interview released by Wikileakes shows "quid pro quo" in Crooked Hillary e-mail probe.Such a dishonest person - &

Paul Ryan does zilch! 16 Oct 2016 22:15

Voter fraud! Crooked Hillary Clinton even got the questions to a debate and nobody says a word. Can you imagine if I got the questions? 17 Oct 2016 15:24

Crooked Hillary colluded w/FBI and DOJ and media is covering up to protect her. It's a #RiggedSystem! Our country d... 17 Oct 2016 21:03

Get rich quick! Crooked Hillary Clinton's pay to play guide: 17 Oct 2016 22:51

Crooked Hillary has never created a job in her life. We will create 25 million jobs. Think she can do that? Not a c... 20 Oct 2016 1:51

Why didn't Hillary Clinton announce that she was inappropriately given the debate questions - she secretly used them! Crooked Hillary. 20 Oct 2016 14:55

Want access to Crooked Hillary? Don't forget - it's going to cost you!#DrainTheSwamp #PayToPlay 20 Oct 2016 18:25

Crooked Hillary promised 200k jobs in NY and FAILED. We'll create 25M jobs when I'm president and I will DELIVER! 20 Oct 2016 20:30

{Crooked Hillary Clinton} created this mess and she knows it. #DrainTheSwamp 21 Oct 2016 22:30

Crooked Hillary Clinton Tops Middle East Forum's 'Islamist Money List' 22 Oct 2016 17:54

If you can't run your own house you certainly can't run the White House A statement made by Mrs. Obama about Crooked Hillary Clinton 23 Oct 2016 12:53

Wow just came out on secret tape that Crooked Hillary wants to take in as many Syrians as possible. We cannot let this happen - ISIS! 24 Oct 2016 12:00

Crooked Hillary launched her political career by letting terrorists off the hook. #DrainTheSwamp... 27 Oct 2016 22:37

Look at the way Crooked Hillary is handling the e-mail case and the total mess she is in. She is unfit to be president. Bad judgement! 1 Nov 2016 10:31

Wow now leading in @ABC /@washingtonpost Poll 46 to 45. Gone up 12 points in two weeks mostly before the Crooked Hillary blow-up! 1 Nov 2016 11:55

Crooked Hillary should not be allowed to run for president. She deleted 33000 e-mails AFTER getting a subpoena from U.S. Congress. RIGGED! 1 Nov 2016 12:01

Crooked Hillary Clinton deleted 33000 e-mails AFTER they were subpoenaed by the United States Congress. Guilty - cannot run. Rigged system! 2 Nov 2016 12:47

After decades of lies and scandal Crooked Hillary's corruption is closing in. #DrainTheSwamp! 2 Nov 2016 19:09

Hey Missouri let's defeat Crooked Hillary & @koster4missouri! Koster supports Obamacare & amnesty! Vote outsider Navy SEAL @EricGreitens! 7 Nov 2016 22:21

Crooked Hillary Clinton now blames everybody but herself refuses to say she was a terrible candidate. Hits Facebook & even Dems & DNC. 1 Jun 2017 0:40

...and did not want to "rock the boat." He didn't "choke" he colluded or obstructed and it did the Dems and Crooked Hillary no good. 26 Jun 2017 12:50

My son Donald openly gave his e-mails to the media & authorities whereas Crooked Hillary Clinton deleted (& acid washed) her 33000 e-mails! 22 Jul 2017 12:00

So why aren't the Committees and investigators and of course our beleaguered A.G. looking into Crooked Hillarys crimes & Russia relations? 24 Jul 2017 12:49

I want to thank Steve Bannon for his service. He came to the campaign during my run against Crooked Hillary Clinton - it was great! Thanks S 19 Aug 2017 11:33

Crooked Hillary Clinton blames everybody (and every thing) but herself for her election loss. She lost the debates and lost her direction! 14 Sep 2017 2:47

After allowing North Korea to research and build Nukes while Secretary of State (Bill C also) Crooked Hillary now criticizes. 20 Sep 2017 10:40

The Russia hoax continues now it's ads on Facebook. What about the totally biased and dishonest Media coverage in favor of Crooked Hillary? 22 Sep 2017 10:44

The greatest influence over our election was the Fake News Media "screaming" for Crooked Hillary Clinton. Next she was a bad candidate! 22 Sep 2017 11:26

I was recently asked if Crooked Hillary Clinton is going to run in 2020? My answer was "I hope so!" 16 Oct 2017 13:12

Wow FBI confirms report that James Comey drafted letter exonerating Crooked Hillary Clinton long before investigation was complete. Many.. 18 Oct 2017 10:21

Crooked Hillary Clinton spent hundreds of millions of dollars more on Presidential Election than I did. Facebook was on her side not mine! 21 Oct 2017 21:21

Sorry but this is years ago before Paul Manafort was part of the Trump campaign. But why aren't Crooked Hillary & the Dems the focus????? 30 Oct 2017 14:25

Everybody is asking why the Justice Department (and FBI) isn't looking into all of the dishonesty going on with Crooked Hillary & the Dems.. 3 Nov 2017 10:57

The real story on Collusion is in Donna B's new book. Crooked Hillary bought the DNC & then stole the Democratic Primary from Crazy Bernie! 3 Nov 2017 11:48

Pocahontas just stated that the Democrats lead by the legendary Crooked Hillary Clinton rigged the Primaries! Lets go FBI & Justice Dept. 3 Nov 2017 11:55

Bernie Sanders supporters have every right to be apoplectic of the complete theft of the Dem primary by Crooked Hillary! 3 Nov 2017 14:28

Does the Fake News Media remember when Crooked Hillary Clinton as Secretary of State was begging Russia to be our friend with the misspelled reset button? Obama tried also but he had zero chemistry with Putin. 12 Nov 2017 0:43

Crooked Hillary Clinton is the worst (and biggest) loser of all time. She just can't stop which is so good for the Republican Party. Hillary get on with your life and give it another try in three years! 18 Nov 2017 13:31

Another Crooked Hillary Fan! 22 Nov 2017 11:08

Charles McCullough the respected fmr Intel Comm Inspector General said public was misled on Crooked Hillary Emails. "Emails endangered National Security." Why aren't our deep State authorities looking at this? Rigged & corrupt? @TuckerCarlson @seanhannity 29 Nov 2017 2:45

"Had the information (Crooked Hillary's emails) been released there would have been harm to National Security...."Charles McCulloughFmr Intel Comm Inspector General 30 Nov 2017 2:00

So General Flynn lies to the FBI and his life is destroyed while Crooked Hillary Clinton on that now famous FBI holiday "interrogation" with no swearing in and no recording lies many times...and nothing happens to her? Rigged system or just a double standard? 3 Dec 2017 2:06

Many people in our Country are asking what the "Justice" Department is going to do about the fact that totally Crooked Hillary AFTER receiving a subpoena from the United States Congress deleted and "acid washed" 33000 Emails? No justice! 3 Dec 2017 2:13

WOW @foxandfrlends "Dossier is bogus. Clinton Campaign DNC funded Dossier. FBI CANNOT (after all of this time) VERIFY CLAIMS IN DOSSIER OF RUSSIA/TRUMP COLLUSION. FBI TAINTED." And they used this Crooked Hillary pile of garbage as the basis for going after the Trump Campaign! 26 Dec 2017 13:24

If the Dems (Crooked Hillary) got elected your stocks would be down 50% from values on Election Day. Now they have a great future - and just beginning! 31 Dec 2017 13:26

Disproven and paid for by Democrats "Dossier used to spy on Trump Campaign. Did FBI use Intel tool to influence the Election?" @foxandfriends Did Dems or Clinton also pay Russians? Where are hidden and smashed DNC servers? Where are Crooked Hillary Emails? What a mess! 11 Jan 2018 11:33

Wow! -Senator Mark Warner got caught having extensive contact with a lobbyist for a Russian oligarch. Warner did not want a "paper trail" on a "private" meeting (in London) he requested with Steele of fraudulent Dossier fame. All tied into Crooked Hillary. 9 Feb 2018 3:22

Now that Adam Schiff is starting to blame President Obama for Russian meddling in the election he is probably doing so as yet another excuse that the Democrats lead by their fearless leader Crooked Hillary Clinton lost the 2016 election. But wasn't I a great candidate? 18 Feb 2018 12:43

....The President Obama quote just before election. That's because he thought Crooked Hillary was going to win and he didn't want to "rock the boat." When I easily won the Electoral College the whole game changed and the Russian excuse became the narrative of the Dems. 20 Feb 2018 12:46

...have shown conclusively that there was no Collusion with Russia..just excuse for losing. The only Collusion was that done by the DNC the Democrats and Crooked Hillary. The writer of the story Maggie Haberman a Hillary flunky knows nothing about me and is not given access. 11 Mar 2018 13:50

The Mueller probe should never have been started in that there was no collusion and there was no crime. It was based on fraudulent activities and a Fake Dossier paid for by Crooked Hillary and the DNC and improperly used in FISA COURT for surveillance of my campaign. WITCH HUNT! 18 Mar 2018 0:12

Why does the Mueller team have 13 hardened Democrats some big Crooked Hillary supporters and Zero Republicans? Another Dem recently added...does anyone think this is fair? And yet there is NO COLLUSION! 18 Mar 2018 12:35

Remember when they were saying during the campaign that Donald Trump is giving great speeches and drawing big crowds but he is spending much less money and not using social media as well as Crooked Hillary's large and highly sophisticated staff. Well not saying that anymore! 22 Mar 2018 10:40

....lawyer or law firm will take months to get up to speed (if for no other reason than they can bill more) which is unfair to our great country - and I am very happy with my existing team. Besides there was NO COLLUSION with Russia except by Crooked Hillary and the Dems! 25 Mar 2018 11:49

....untruthful slime ball who was as time has proven a terrible Director of the FBI. His handling of the Crooked Hillary Clinton case and the events surrounding it will go down as one of the worst "botch jobs" of history. It was my great honor to fire James Comey! 13 Apr 2018 12:17

Unbelievably James Comey states that Polls where Crooked

Hillary was leading were a factor in the handling (stupidly) of the Clinton Email probe. In other words he was making decisions based on the fact that he thought she was going to win and he wanted a job. Slimeball! 15 Apr 2018 11:42

Comey drafted the Crooked Hillary exoneration long before he talked to her (lied in Congress to Senator G) then based his decisions on her poll numbers. Disgruntled he McCabe and the others committed many crimes! 16 Apr 2018 12:25

Why isn't disgraced FBI official Andrew McCabe being investigated for the $700000 Crooked Hillary Democrats in Virginia led by Clinton best friend Terry M (under FBI investigation that they killed) gave to McCabe's wife in her run for office? Then dropped case on Clinton! 18 May 2018 13:38

...Follow the money! The spy was there early in the campaign and yet never reported Collusion with Russia because there was no Collusion. He was only there to spy for political reasons and to help Crooked Hillary win - just like they did to Bernie Sanders who got duped! 23 May 2018 1:13

This whole Russia Probe is Rigged. Just an excuse as to why the Dems and Crooked Hillary lost the Election and States that haven't been lost in decades. 13 Angry Democrats and all Dems if you include the people who worked for Obama for 8 years. #SPYGATE & CONFLICTS OF INTEREST! 26 May 2018 19:41

Why didn't the 13 Angry Democrats investigate the campaign of Crooked Hillary Clinton many crimes much Collusion with Russia? Why didn't the FBI take the Server from the DNC? Rigged Investigation! 27 May 2018 14:13

Why didn't President Obama do something about the so-called Russian Meddling when he was told about it by the FBI before the Election? Because he thought Crooked Hillary was going to win and he didn't want to upset the apple cart! He was in charge not me and did nothing. 27 May 2018 20:32

Why aren't the 13 Angry and heavily conflicted Democrats investigating the totally Crooked Campaign of totally Crooked Hillary Clinton. It's a Rigged Witch Hunt that's why! Ask them if they enjoyed her after election celebration! 29 May 2018 11:09

What is taking so long with the Inspector General's Report on Crooked Hillary and Slippery James Comey. Numerous delays. Hope Report is not being changed and made weaker! There are so many horrible things to tell the public has the right to know. Transparency! 5 Jun 2018 10:38

Wow what a tough sentence for Paul Manafort who has represented Ronald Reagan Bob Dole and many other top political people and campaigns. Didn't know Manafort was the head of the Mob. What about Comey and Crooked Hillary and all of the others? Very unfair! 15 Jun 2018 17:41

WITCH HUNT! There was no Russian Collusion. Oh I see there was no Russian Collusion so now they look for obstruction on the no Russian Collusion. The phony Russian Collusion was a made up Hoax. Too bad they didn't look at Crooked Hillary like this. Double Standard! 17 Jun 2018 14:54

Why was the FBI's sick loser Peter Strzok working on the totally discredited Mueller team of 13 Angry & Conflicted Democrats when Strzok was giving Crooked Hillary a free pass yet telling his lover lawyer Lisa Page that "we'll stop" Trump from becoming President? Witch Hunt! 18 Jun 2018 0:42

The face of the Democrats is now Maxine Waters who together with Nancy Pelosi have established a fine leadership team. They should always stay together and lead the Democrats who want Open Borders and Unlimited Crime well into the future....and pick Crooked Hillary for Pres. 26 Jun 2018 12:36

....persecuted on old and/or totally unrelated charges (there was no collusion and there was no obstruction of the no collusion)...And what is going on in the FBI & DOJ with Crooked Hillary the DNC and all of the lies? A disgraceful situation! 28 Jun 2018 12:56

The Rigged Witch Hunt originally headed by FBI lover boy Peter S (for one year) & now 13 Angry Democrats should look into the missing DNC Server Crooked Hillary's illegally deleted Emails the Pakistani Fraudster Uranium One Podesta & so much more. It's a Democrat Con Job! 7 Jul 2018 22:24

These Russian individuals did their work during the Obama years. Why didn't Obama do something about it? Because he thought Crooked Hillary Clinton would win that's why. Had nothing to do with the Trump Administration but Fake News doesn't want to report the truth as usual! 14 Jul 2018 18:17

President Obama thought that Crooked Hillary was going to

win the election so when he was informed by the FBI about Russian Meddling he said it couldn't happen was no big deal & did NOTHING about it. When I won it became a big deal and the Rigged Witch Hunt headed by Strzok! 16 Jul 2018 5:37

Looking more & more like the Trump Campaign for President was illegally being spied upon (surveillance) for the political gain of Crooked Hillary Clinton and the DNC. Ask her how that worked out - she did better with Crazy Bernie. Republicans must get tough now. An illegal Scam! 22 Jul 2018 10:49

So President Obama knew about Russia before the Election. Why didn't he do something about it? Why didn't he tell our campaign? Because it is all a big hoax that's why and he thought Crooked Hillary was going to win!!! 22 Jul 2018 22:23

So we now find out that it was indeed the unverified and Fake Dirty Dossier that was paid for by Crooked Hillary Clinton and the DNC that was knowingly & falsely submitted to FISA and which was responsible for starting the totally conflicted and discredited Mueller Witch Hunt! 23 Jul 2018 10:30

.....I did NOT know of the meeting with my son Don jr. Sounds to me like someone is trying to make up stories in order to get himself out of an unrelated jam (Taxi cabs maybe?). He even retained Bill and Crooked Hillary's lawyer. Gee I wonder if they helped him make the choice! 27 Jul 2018 11:56

There is No Collusion! The Robert Mueller Rigged Witch Hunt headed now by 17 (increased from 13 including an Obama White House lawyer) Angry Democrats was started by a fraudulent Dossier paid for by Crooked Hillary and the DNC. Therefore the Witch Hunt is an illegal Scam! 29 Jul 2018 19:35

....Also why is Mueller only appointing Angry Dems some of whom have worked for Crooked Hillary others including himself have worked for Obama....And why isn't Mueller looking at all of the criminal activity & real Russian Collusion on the Democrats side-Podesta Dossier? 29 Jul 2018 20:20

Collusion is not a crime but that doesn't matter because there was No Collusion (except by Crooked Hillary and the Democrats)! 31 Jul 2018 11:58

This is an illegally brought Rigged Witch Hunt run by people who are totally corrupt and/or conflicted. It was started and paid for by Crooked Hillary and the Democrats. Phony Dossier FISA disgrace and so many lying and dishonest people already fired. 17 Angry Dems? Stay tuned! 9 Aug 2018 16:02

The big story that the Fake News Media refuses to report is lowlife Christopher Steele's many meetings with Deputy A.G. Bruce Ohr and his beautiful wife Nelly. It was Fusion GPS that hired Steele to write the phony & discredited Dossier paid for by Crooked Hillary & the DNC.... 11 Aug 2018 18:28

Just fired Agent Strzok formerly of the FBI was in charge of the Crooked Hillary Clinton sham investigation. It was a total fraud on the American public and should be properly redone! 13 Aug 2018 16:09

Fired FBI Agent Peter Strzok is a fraud as is the rigged investigation he started. There was no Collusion or Obstruction with Russia and everybody including the Democrats know it. The only Collusion and Obstruction was by Crooked Hillary the Democrats and the DNC! 14 Aug 2018 13:01

Strzok started the illegal Rigged Witch Hunt - why isn't this so-called "probe" ended immediately? Why aren't these angry and conflicted Democrats instead looking at Crooked Hillary? 14 Aug 2018 13:10

No Collusion and No Obstruction except by Crooked Hillary and the Democrats. All of the resignations and corruption yet heavily conflicted Bob Mueller refuses to even look in that direction. What about the Brennan Comey McCabe Strzok lies to Congress or Crooked's Emails! 19 Aug 2018 11:30

The only thing that I have done wrong is to win an election that was expected to be won by Crooked Hillary Clinton and the Democrats. The problem is they forgot to campaign in numerous states! 23 Aug 2018 0:56

Big story out that the FBI ignored tens of thousands of Crooked Hillary Emails many of which are REALLY BAD. Also gave false election info. I feel sure that we will soon be getting to the bottom of all of this corruption. At some point I may have to get involved! 25 Aug 2018 13:05

"The FBI only looked at 3000 of 675000 Crooked Hillary Clinton Emails." They purposely didn't look at the disasters. This news is just out. @FoxNews 25 Aug 2018 13:11

Universities will someday study what highly conflicted (and NOT Senate approved) Bob Mueller and his gang of Democrat thugs have done to destroy people. Why is he protecting Crooked Hillary Comey McCabe Lisa Page & her lover Peter S and all of his friends on the other side? 15 Nov 2018 14:49

The Mueller Witch Hunt is a total disgrace. They are looking at supposedly stolen Crooked Hillary Clinton Emails (even though they don't want to look at the DNC Server) but have no interest in the Emails that Hillary DELETED & acid washed AFTER getting a Congressional Subpoena! 28 Nov 2018 0:31

Did you ever see an investigation more in search of a crime? At the same time Mueller and the Angry Democrats aren't even looking at the atrocious and perhaps subversive crimes that were committed by Crooked Hillary Clinton and the Democrats. A total disgrace! 29 Nov 2018 11:54

.....overturned 9-0 in the United States Supreme Court. Doing same thing to people now. Will all of the substantial & many contributions made by the 17 Angry Democrats to the Campaign of Crooked Hillary be listed in top of Report. Will the people that worked for the Clinton.... 7 Dec 2018 11:40

....WILL NEVER BE PROVEN AND ARE LIKELY FALSE." Thank you to Michael Isikoff Yahoo for honesty. What this means is that the FISA WARRANTS and the whole Russian Witch Hunt is a Fraud and a Hoax which should be ended immediately. Also it was paid for by Crooked Hillary & DNC! 18 Dec 2018 13:22

Build that Wall

My persona will never be that of a wallflower - I'd rather build walls than cling to them --Donald J. Trump 12 May 2009 14:07

Illegal immigration is a wrecking ball aimed at US taxpayers. Washington needs to get tough and fight for "W... (cont) 6 Dec 2011 16:22

No surprise with the talk of amnesty in DC illegal immigration is picking up in Arizona 14 Feb 2013 21:24

Congress must protect our borders first. Amnesty should be done only if the border is secure and illegal immigration has stopped. 29 Aug 2013 18:08

Central American presidents are blaming us for the influx of illegal immigration Obama will soon apologize. 28 Jul 2014 21:08

SECURE THE BORDER! BUILD A WALL! 5 Aug 2014 20:34

The fight against ISIS starts at our border. 'At least' 10 ISIS have been caught crossing the Mexico border. Build a wall! 8 Oct 2014 21:26

Via @BreitbartNews: "DONALD TRUMP: EXEC AMNESTY WILL MAKE ILLEGAL IMMIGRATION 'WORSE THAN IT'S EVER BEEN" 28 Feb 2015 18:30

Mexico's court system   corrupt.I want nothing to do with Mexico other than to build an impenetrable WALL and stop them from ripping off U.S. 6 Mar 2015 0:50

The border is wide open for cartels & terrorists. Secure our border now. Build a massive wall & deduct the costs from Mexican foreign aid! 30 Mar 2015 20:47

Our border is being breached daily by criminals. We must build a wall & deduct costs from Mexican foreign aid! 16 Apr 2015 14:50

ISIS is operating a training camp 8 miles outside our Southern border. We need a wall. Deduct costs from Mexico! 17 Apr

2015 13:17

My @TheBrodyFile int. from Iowa on how I would build a wall to secure our Southern Border & deduct costs from Mexico 20 May 2015 20:22

Wouldn't it be nice if our government could build a wall on the border under budget and ahead of schedule?! - my @SRQRepublicans speech. 21 May 2015 23:50

Via @G_Liberty_Voice by Melody Dareing: "Donald Trump Wants to Build a Wall Between U.S. And Mexico" 1 Jun 2015 16:45

Just made the point at #NCGOPcon that "we have to protect our border & I think everyone here knows nobody can build a wall like Trump!" 7 Jun 2015 0:03

We MUST have strong borders and stop illegal immigration. Without that we do not have a country. Also Mexico is killing U.S. on trade. WIN! 30 Jun 2015 12:35

My recent statement re: @macys -- We must have strong borders & stop illegal immigration now!... 1 Jul 2015 15:21

Those who believe in tight border security stopping illegal immigration & SMART trade deals w/other countries should boycott @Macys. 1 Jul 2015 16:59

For all of those who want to #MakeAmericaGreatAgain boycott @Macys. They are weak on border security & stopping illegal immigration. 1 Jul 2015 17:00

Make our borders strong and stop illegal immigration. Even President Obama agrees- 1 Jul 2015 22:27

A country must enforce its borders. Respect for the rule of law is at our country's core. We must build a wall! 2 Jul 2015 19:24

Where are the other candidates now that this tragic murder has taken place b/c of our unsafe border. We need a wall! 3 Jul 2015 22:44

Via @CNNPolitics by @teddyschleifer: "Trump: San Francisco killing shows perils of illegal immigration" 4 Jul 2015 2:59

@CNNPolitics: Trump: San Francisco killing shows perils of illegal immigration (via @TeddySchleifer) 4 Jul 2015 3:38

@myGianLuca: @CNNPolitics @teddyschleifer Say it LOUD & PROUD @realDonaldTrump! *** ILLEGAL IMMIGRATION *** Is an Attack on Our Country! 4 Jul 2015 3:48

Miss Universe Paulina Vega criticized me for telling the truth about illegal immigration but then said she would keep the crown-Hypocrite 5 Jul 2015 8:57

@greta just read @realDonaldTrump going to Phoenix to give speech on illegal immigration on Saturday That is correct. I look forward to it 8 Jul 2015 19:26

BREAKING - Border security rally in Phoenix AZ at 2PM MST has been moved to @PhoenixConvCtr! Build a wall! Let's Make America Great Again! 10 Jul 2015 1:55

Today I am standing with patriots in Arizona for border security! Build a wall! Let's Make America Great Again! 11 Jul 2015 16:55

Legal immigrants want border security. It is common sense. We must build a wall! Let's Make America Great Again! 11 Jul 2015 19:06

@WayneDupreeShow: Aren't U angry how the media has turned DonaldTrump SLAM against illegal immigration" into him hating "all immigrants 11 Jul 2015 11:52

A nation without borders is no nation at all. We must build a wall. Let's Make America Great Again! 14 Jul 2015 13:40

John McCain called thousands of people "crazies" when they came to seek help on illegal immigration last week in Phoenix. He owes apology! 19 Jul 2015 10:15

I will be interviewed on @oreillyfactor tonight at 8:00. Will be talking about the poor treatment of our veterans illegal immigration etc. 20 Jul 2015 23:27

Good luck to my new friends on your testimony in DC. You are amazing people doing something so important--- stopping illegal immigration! 21 Jul 2015 14:14

Isn't it amazing that @Macys paid a massive fine for profiling African Americans--& then criticized me for discussing illegal immigration! 24 Jul 2015 20:46

We must build a wall to secure our border. It will save lives and help Make America Great Again! 27 Jul 2015 19:44

Again illegal immigrant is charged with the fatal bludgeoning of a wonderful and loved 64 year old woman. Get them out and build a WALL! 11 Aug 2015 0:29

We must stop the crime and killing machine that is illegal immigration. Rampant problems will only get worse. Take back our country! 11 Aug 2015 0:58

Now that I started my war on illegal immigration and securing the border most other candidates are finally speaking up. Just politicians! 22 Aug 2015 21:22

For those that don't think a wall (fence) works why don't they suggest taking down the fence around the White House? Foolish people! 31 Aug 2015 15:05

I spell out some of the differences between Ben Carson and myself at 9:00 A.M. on @CNN @jaketapper. Ben is very weak on illegal immigration. 25 Oct 2015 11:34

Anybody that believes in strong borders and stopping illegal immigration cannot vote for Marco Rubio 1 Nov 2015 12:40

@wakeupfla: Please stand up for American Hispanic families and fight illegal immigration it is destroying USA! 8 Nov 2015 12:19

Marco Rubio is totally weak on illegal immigration & in favor of easy amnesty. A lightweight choker - bad for #USA! 10 Nov 2015 3:39

Wow pres. candidate Ben Carson who is very weak on illegal Immigration just said he likes amnesty and a pathway to citizenship. 12 Nov 2015 19:21

Macy's was very disloyal to me bc of my strong stance on illegal immigration. Their stock has crashed! #BoycottMacys 12 Nov 2015 21:05

Eight Syrians were just caught on the southern border trying to get into the U.S. ISIS maybe? I told you so. WE NEED A BIG & BEAUTIFUL WALL! 19 Nov 2015 13:11

Everyone is now saying how right I was with illegal immigration & the wall. After Paris they're all on the bandwagon. 19 Nov 2015 16:30

.@HillaryClinton is weak on illegal immigration & totally incompetent as a manager and leader - no strength or stamina to be #POTUS! 20 Nov 2015 21:38

13 Syrian refugees were caught trying to get into the U.S. through the Southern Border. How many made it? WE NEED THE WALL! 22 Nov 2015 15:53

Hillary Clinton is weak on illegal immigration among many other things. She is strong on corruption - corruption is what she's best at! 22 Nov 2015 22:56

When you do your Christmas shopping remember how disloyal @Macys was to the subject of illegal immigration. #BoycottMacys #DumpMacys 23 Nov 2015 18:45

@Blacks4Trump16: Legal & illegal immigration drive down American wages. Only DonaldTrump can fix this. @AnnCoulter #Trump2016 #TeamTrump 2 Dec 2015 23:48

When will the Democrats and Hillary in particular say "we must build a wall a great wall and Mexico is going to pay for it?" Never! 25 Dec 2015 20:45

Hillary Clinton said that it is O.K. to ban Muslims from Israel by building a WALL but not O.K. to do so in the U.S. We must be vigilant! 2 Jan 2016 13:23

.@AnnCoulter has been amazing. We will win and establish strong borders we will build a WALL and Mexico will pay. We will be great again! 23 Jan 2016 14:45

I told you so. Our country totally lost control of illegal immigration even with criminals. 6 Feb 2016 2:42

We will stop heroin and other drugs from coming into New Hampshire from our open southern border. We will build a WALL and have security. 9 Feb 2016 22:19

I will end illegal immigration and protect our borders! We need to MAKE AMERICA SAFE & GREAT AGAIN! #Trump2016 13 Feb 2016 0:31

RT @TomOdell: .@FoxNews - Pope who lives in a Vatican city fortified with huge walls thinks it's wrong to build walls? Really? 18 Feb 2016 19:42

RT @benshapiro: Pope on Trump: "A person who thinks only about building walls...is not Christian." This is Vatican City. 18 Feb 2016 19:42

RT @JoeNBC: "Pope Francis tear down that wall!"#vaticanwalls 19 Feb 2016 0:05

FMR PRES of Mexico Vicente Fox horribly used the F word when discussing the wall. He must apologize! If I did that there would be a uproar! 25 Feb 2016 20:27

I will bring our jobs back to America fix our military and take care of our vets end Common Core and ObamaCare protect 2nd A build WALL 15 Mar 2016 10:25

It is amazing how often I am right only to be criticized by the media. Illegal immigration take the oil build the wall Muslims NATO! 24 Mar 2016 14:38

We must build a great wall between Mexico and the United States! 1 Apr 2016 21:49

Obama says a WALL at our southern border won't enhance our security (wrong) and yet he now wants to build a much bigger wall (fence) at W.H. 30 May 2016 10:41

In getting the endorsement of the 16500 Border Patrol Agents (thank you) the statement was made that the WALL was very necessary! 30 May 2016 11:00

Obama & Clinton should stop meeting with special interests & start meeting with the victims of illegal immigration. 23 Jun 2016 18:30

New GOP platform now includes language that supports the border wall. We will build the wall and MAKE AMERICA SAFE AGAIN! 13 Jul 2016 21:56

Will be on #Hannity @ 10pE @FoxNews- discussing various subjects including immigration-if elected we will #BuildTheWall & enforce our laws! 25 Aug 2016 0:05

I am very proud to have brought the subject of illegal immigration back into the discussion. Such a big problem for our country-I will solve 26 Aug 2016 16:01

Heroin overdoses are taking over our children and others in the MIDWEST. Coming in from our southern border. We need strong border & WALL! 27 Aug 2016 14:17

I will be making a major speech on ILLEGAL IMMIGRATION on Wednesday in the GREAT State of Arizona. Big crowds looking for a larger venue. 28 Aug 2016 23:27

From day one I said that I was going to build a great wall on the SOUTHERN BORDER and much more. Stop illegal immigration. Watch Wednesday! 30 Aug 2016 10:27

Mexico will pay for the wall - 100%!#MakeAmericaGreatAgain #ImWithYou 1 Sep 2016 4:58

Mexico will pay for the wall! 1 Sep 2016 10:31

The Republican Party needs strong and committed leaders not weak people such as @JeffFlake if it is going to stop illegal immigration. 4 Sep 2016 22:05

Paul Ryan should spend more time on balancing the budget jobs and illegal immigration and not waste his time on fighting Republican nominee 10 Oct 2016 17:22

Thank you NH! We will end illegal immigration stop the drugs deport all criminal aliens&save American lives! 4 Nov 2016 18:46

The dishonest media does not report that any money spent on building the Great Wall (for sake of speed) will be paid back by Mexico later! 6 Jan 2017 11:19

Dishonest media says Mexico won't be paying for the wall if they pay a little later so the wall can be built more quickly. Media is fake! 9 Jan 2017 4:05

Big day planned on NATIONAL SECURITY tomorrow. Among many other things we will build the wall! 25 Jan 2017 2:37

of jobs and companies lost. If Mexico is unwilling to pay for the badly needed wall then it would be better to cancel the upcoming meeting. 26 Jan 2017 13:55

...Senators should focus their energies on ISIS illegal immigration and border security instead of always looking to start World War III. 29 Jan 2017 21:49

I am reading that the great border WALL will cost more than the government originally thought but I have not gotten involved in the..... 11 Feb 2017 13:18

Jobs are returning illegal immigration is plummeting law order and justice are being restored. We are truly making America great again! 13 Apr 2017 0:32

The super Liberal Democrat in the Georgia Congressioal race

tomorrow wants to protect criminals allow illegal immigration and raise taxes! 17 Apr 2017 13:31

The weak illegal immigration policies of the Obama Admin. allowed bad MS 13 gangs to form in cities across U.S. We are removing them fast! 18 Apr 2017 9:39

Democrat Jon Ossoff would be a disaster in Congress. VERY weak on crime and illegal immigration bad for jobs and wants higher taxes. Say NO 18 Apr 2017 10:38

The Democrats don't want money from budget going to border wall despite the fact that it will stop drugs and very bad MS 13 gang members. 23 Apr 2017 15:42

Eventually but at a later date so we can get started early Mexico will be paying in some form for the badly needed border wall. 23 Apr 2017 15:44

The Wall is a very important tool in stopping drugs from pouring into our country and poisoning our youth (and many others)! If 24 Apr 2017 12:28

....the wall is not built which it will be the drug situation will NEVER be fixed the way it should be!#BuildTheWall 24 Apr 2017 15:31

Don't let the fake media tell you that I have changed my position on the WALL. It will get built and help stop drugs human trafficking etc. 25 Apr 2017 12:36

Mexico was just ranked the second deadliest country in the world after only Syria. Drug trade is largely the cause. We will BUILD THE WALL! 22 Jun 2017 22:15

Big WIN today for building the wall. It will secure the border & save lives. Now the full House & Senate must act! 12 Jul 2017 23:24

Luther Strange of the Great State of Alabama has my endorsement. He is strong on Border & Wall the military tax cuts & law enforcement. 14 Aug 2017 10:38

Wow Senator Luther Strange picked up a lot of additional support since my endorsement. Now in September runoff. Strong on Wall & Crime! 16 Aug 2017 14:51

With Mexico being one of the highest crime Nations in the world we must have THE WALL. Mexico will pay for it through reimbursement/other. 27 Aug 2017 13:44

The WALL which is already under construction in the form of new renovation of old and existing fences and walls will continue to be built. 14 Sep 2017 10:20

The Democrats want MASSIVE tax increases & soft crime producing borders.The Republicans want the biggest tax cut in history & the WALL! 11 Oct 2017 10:36

BORDER WALL prototypes underway! 17 Oct 2017 23:03

I am leaving China for #APEC2017 in Vietnam. @FLOTUS Melania is staying behind to see the zoo and of course the Great WALL of China before going to Alaska to greet our AMAZING troops. 10 Nov 2017 1:17

Border Patrol Officer killed at Southern Border another badly hurt. We will seek out and bring to justice those responsible. We will and must build the Wall! 20 Nov 2017 1:29

HAPPY THANKSGIVING your Country is starting to do really well. Jobs coming back highest Stock Market EVER Military getting really strong we will build the WALL V.A. taking care of our Vets great Supreme Court Justice RECORD CUT IN REGS lowest unemployment in 17 years....! 23 Nov 2017 11:28

Will be calling the President of Egypt in a short while to discuss the tragic terrorist attack with so much loss of life. We have to get TOUGHER AND SMARTER than ever before and we will. Need the WALL need the BAN! God bless the people of Egypt. 24 Nov 2017 18:49

After North Korea missile launch it's more important than ever to fund our gov't & military! Dems shouldn't hold troop funding hostage for amnesty & illegal immigration. I ran on stopping illegal immigration and won big. They can't now threaten a shutdown to get their demands. 29 Nov 2017 1:45

The Kate Steinle killer came back and back over the weakly protected Obama border always committing crimes and being violent and yet this info was not used in court. His exoneration is a complete travesty of justice. BUILD THE WALL! 1 Dec 2017 11:03

A disgraceful verdict in the Kate Steinle case! No wonder the people of our Country are so angry with Illegal Immigration. 1 Dec 2017 3:30

Democrats refusal to give even one vote for massive Tax Cuts is why we need Republican Roy Moore to win in Alabama. We need his vote on stopping crime illegal immigration Border Wall Military Pro Life V.A. Judges 2nd Amendment and more. No to Jones a Pelosi/Schumer Puppet! 4 Dec 2017 11:17

RT @Scavino45: Time lapse video of the border wall prototypes when they were being built in San Diego. Next phase underway: testing and ev... 6 Dec 2017 12:53

The people of Alabama will do the right thing. Doug Jones is Pro-Abortion weak on Crime Military and Illegal Immigration Bad for Gun Owners and Veterans and against the WALL. Jones is a Pelosi/Schumer Puppet. Roy Moore will always vote with us. VOTE ROY MOORE! 12 Dec 2017 14:09

The Democrats have been told and fully understand that there can be no DACA without the desperately needed WALL at the Southern Border and an END to the horrible Chain Migration & ridiculous Lottery System of Immigration etc. We must protect our Country at all cost! 29 Dec 2017 13:16

As I made very clear today our country needs the security of the Wall on the Southern Border which must be part of any DACA approval. 10 Jan 2018 0:16

The United States needs the security of the Wall on the Southern Border which must be part of any DACA approval. The safety and security of our country is #1! 10 Jan 2018 23:07

"45 year low in illegal immigration this year." @foxandfriends 11 Jan 2018 13:11

The Democrats seem intent on having people and drugs pour into our country from the Southern Border risking thousands of lives in the process. It is my duty to protect the lives and safety of all Americans. We must build a Great Wall think Merit and end Lottery & Chain. USA! 12 Jan 2018 4:42

The so-called bipartisan DACA deal presented yesterday to myself and a group of Republican Senators and Congressmen was a big step backwards. Wall was not properly funded Chain & Lottery were made worse and USA would be forced to take large numbers of people from high crime..... 12 Jan 2018 11:59

We must have Security at our VERY DANGEROUS SOUTHERN

BORDER and we must have a great WALL to help protect us and to help stop the massive inflow of drugs pouring into our country! 16 Jan 2018 13:54

The Wall is the Wall it has never changed or evolved from the first day I conceived of it. Parts will be of necessity see through and it was never intended to be built in areas where there is natural protection such as mountains wastelands or tough rivers or water..... 18 Jan 2018 11:15

....The Wall will be paid for directly or indirectly or through longer term reimbursement by Mexico which has a ridiculous $71 billion dollar trade surplus with the U.S. The $20 billion dollar Wall is "peanuts" compared to what Mexico makes from the U.S. NAFTA is a bad joke! 18 Jan 2018 11:25

We need the Wall for the safety and security of our country. We need the Wall to help stop the massive inflow of drugs from Mexico now rated the number one most dangerous country in the world. If there is no Wall there is no Deal! 18 Jan 2018 13:16

Government Funding Bill past last night in the House of Representatives. Now Democrats are needed if it is to pass in the Senate - but they want illegal immigration and weak borders. Shutdown coming? We need more Republican victories in 2018! 19 Jan 2018 12:04

Democrats are holding our Military hostage over their desire to have unchecked illegal immigration. Can't let that happen! 20 Jan 2018 14:27

RT @realDonaldTrump: Democrats are holding our Military hostage over their desire to have unchecked illegal immigration. Can't let that hap... 21 Jan 2018 12:20

Cryin' Chuck Schumer fully understands especially after his humiliating defeat that if there is no Wall there is no DACA. We must have safety and security together with a strong Military for our great people! 24 Jan 2018 4:07

Thank you to Brandon Judd of the National Border Patrol Council for his strong statement on @foxandfriends that we very badly NEED THE WALL. Must also end loophole of "catch & release" and clean up the legal and other procedures at the border NOW for Safety & Security reasons. 27 Jan 2018 11:55

Any deal on DACA that does not include STRONG border security and the desperately needed WALL is a total waste of time. March 5th is rapidly approaching and the Dems seem not to care about DACA. Make a deal! 5 Feb 2018 14:36

So disgraceful that a person illegally in our country killed @Colts linebacker Edwin Jackson. This is just one of many such preventable tragedies. We must get the Dems to get tough on the Border and with illegal immigration FAST! 6 Feb 2018 13:32

The Schumer-Rounds-Collins immigration bill would be a total catastrophe. @DHSgov says it would be "the end of immigration enforcement in America." It creates a giant amnesty (including for dangerous criminals) doesn't build the wall expands chain migration keeps the visa... 15 Feb 2018 19:25

MS-13 gang members are being removed by our Great ICE and Border Patrol Agents by the thousands but these killers come back in from El Salvador and through Mexico like water. El Salvador just takes our money and Mexico must help MORE with this problem. We need The Wall! 23 Feb 2018 11:28

Big legal win today. U.S. judge sided with the Trump Administration and rejected the attempt to stop the government from building a great Border Wall on the Southern Border. Now this important project can go forward! 28 Feb 2018 4:28

I have decided that sections of the Wall that California wants built NOW will not be built until the whole Wall is approved. Big victory yesterday with ruling from the courts that allows us to proceed. OUR COUNTRY MUST HAVE BORDER SECURITY! 28 Feb 2018 12:29

Heading to see the BORDER WALL prototypes in California! 13 Mar 2018 14:37

"According to the Center for Immigration Studies the $18 billion wall will pay for itself by curbing the importation of crime drugs and illegal immigrants who tend to go on the federal dole..." 13 Mar 2018 15:24

If we don't have a wall system we're not going to have a country. Congress must fund the BORDER WALL & prohibit grants to sanctuary jurisdictions that threaten the security of our country & the people of our country. We must enforce our laws & protect our people! #BuildTheWall 13 Mar 2018 22:23

Got $1.6 Billion to start Wall on Southern Border rest will be forthcoming. Most importantly got $700 Billion to rebuild our Military $716 Billion next year...most ever. Had to waste money on Dem giveaways in order to take care of military pay increase and new equipment. 22 Mar 2018 3:00

Democrats refused to take care of DACA. Would have been so easy but they just didn't care. I had to fight for Military and start of Wall. 22 Mar 2018 3:04

DACA was abandoned by the Democrats. Very unfair to them! Would have been tied to desperately needed Wall. 23 Mar 2018 12:26

I am considering a VETO of the Omnibus Spending Bill based on the fact that the 800000 plus DACA recipients have been totally abandoned by the Democrats (not even mentioned in Bill) and the BORDER WALL which is desperately needed for our National Defense is not fully funded. 23 Mar 2018 12:55

Because of the $700 & $716 Billion Dollars gotten to rebuild our Military many jobs are created and our Military is again rich. Building a great Border Wall with drugs (poison) and enemy combatants pouring into our Country is all about National Defense. Build WALL through M! 25 Mar 2018 10:33

Much can be done with the $1.6 Billion given to building and fixing the border wall. It is just a down payment. Work will start immediately. The rest of the money will come - and remember DACA the Democrats abandoned you (but we will not)! 25 Mar 2018 10:42

Great briefing this afternoon on the start of our Southern Border WALL! 28 Mar 2018 19:47

Mexico is doing very little if not NOTHING at stopping people from flowing into Mexico through their Southern Border and then into the U.S. They laugh at our dumb immigration laws. They must stop the big drug and people flows or I will stop their cash cow NAFTA. NEED WALL! 1 Apr 2018 14:25

Border Patrol Agents are not allowed to properly do their job at the Border because of ridiculous liberal (Democrat) laws like Catch & Release. Getting more dangerous. "Caravans" coming. Republicans must go to Nuclear Option to pass tough laws NOW. NO MORE DACA DEAL! 1 Apr 2018 13:56

DACA is dead because the Democrats didn't care or act and

now everyone wants to get onto the DACA bandwagon... No longer works. Must build Wall and secure our borders with proper Border legislation. Democrats want No Borders hence drugs and crime! 2 Apr 2018 11:17

Mexico has the absolute power not to let these large "Caravans" of people enter their country. They must stop them at their Northern Border which they can do because their border laws work not allow them to pass through into our country which has no effective border laws..... 2 Apr 2018 11:02

Honduras Mexico and many other countries that the U.S. is very generous to sends many of their people to our country through our WEAK IMMIGRATION POLICIES. Caravans are heading here. Must pass tough laws and build the WALL. Democrats allow open borders drugs and crime! 3 Apr 2018 0:12

The big Caravan of People from Honduras now coming across Mexico and heading to our "Weak Laws" Border had better be stopped before it gets there. Cash cow NAFTA is in play as is foreign aid to Honduras and the countries that allow this to happen. Congress MUST ACT NOW! 3 Apr 2018 10:49

The Caravan is largely broken up thanks to the strong immigration laws of Mexico and their willingness to use them so as not to cause a giant scene at our Border. Because of the Trump Administrations actions Border crossings are at a still UNACCEPTABLE 46 year low. Stop drugs! 5 Apr 2018 11:40

Tremendous pressure is building like never before for the Border Wall and an end to crime cradling Sanctuary Cities. Started the Wall in San Diego where the people were pushing really hard to get it. They will soon be protected! 13 Apr 2018 11:44

Looks like Jerry Brown and California are not looking for safety and security along their very porous Border. He cannot come to terms for the National Guard to patrol and protect the Border. The high crime rate will only get higher. Much wanted Wall in San Diego already started! 17 Apr 2018 12:24

Despite the Democrat inspired laws on Sanctuary Cities and the Border being so bad and one sided I have instructed the Secretary of Homeland Security not to let these large Caravans of people into our Country. It is a disgrace. We are the only Country in the World so naive! WALL 23 Apr 2018 13:44

Mexico whose laws on immigration are very tough must stop people from going through Mexico and into the U.S. We may make this a condition of the new NAFTA Agreement. Our Country cannot accept what is happening! Also we must get Wall funding fast. 23 Apr 2018 13:51

.@JimRenacci has worked so hard on Tax Reductions Illegal Immigration the Border and Crime. I need Jim very badly to help our agenda and to keep MAKING AMERICA GREAT AGAIN! He will be a fantastic Senator for the Great State of Ohio and has my full endorsement! 24 Apr 2018 19:05

.@JimRenacci has worked so hard on Tax Reductions Illegal Immigration the Border and Crime. I need Jim very badly to help our agenda and to keep MAKING AMERICA GREAT AGAIN! He will be a fantastic Senator for the Great State of Ohio and has my full endorsement! 24 Apr 2018 19:06

The migrant 'caravan' that is openly defying our border shows how weak & ineffective U.S. immigration laws are. Yet Democrats like Jon Tester continue to support the open borders agenda – Tester even voted to protect Sanctuary Cities. We need lawmakers who will put America First. 30 Apr 2018 22:38

Our Southern Border is under siege. Congress must act now to change our weak and ineffective immigration laws. Must build a Wall. Mexico which has a massive crime problem is doing little to help! 4 May 2018 10:22

We are going to demand Congress secure the border in the upcoming CR. Illegal immigration must end! 4 May 2018 21:59

The Senate should get funding done before the August break or NOT GO HOME. Wall and Border Security should be included. Also waiting for approval of almost 300 nominations worst in history. Democrats are doing everything possible to obstruct all they know how to do. STAY! 12 May 2018 22:20

Put pressure on the Democrats to end the horrible law that separates children from there parents once they cross the Border into the U.S. Catch and Release Lottery and Chain must also go with it and we MUST continue building the WALL! DEMOCRATS ARE PROTECTING MS-13 THUGS. 26 May 2018 13:59

Democrats mistakenly tweet 2014 pictures from Obama's

term showing children from the Border in steel cages. They thought it was recent pictures in order to make us look bad but backfires. Dems must agree to Wall and new Border Protection for good of country...Bipartisan Bill! 29 May 2018 10:07

This is my 500th. Day in Office and we have accomplished a lot - many believe more than any President in his first 500 days. Massive Tax & Regulation Cuts Military & Vets Lower Crime & Illegal Immigration Stronger Borders Judgeships Best Economy & Jobs EVER and much more... 4 Jun 2018 11:35

Separating families at the Border is the fault of bad legislation passed by the Democrats. Border Security laws should be changed but the Dems can't get their act together! Started the Wall. 5 Jun 2018 11:58

The Democrats are forcing the breakup of families at the Border with their horrible and cruel legislative agenda. Any Immigration Bill MUST HAVE full funding for the Wall end Catch & Release Visa Lottery and Chain and go to Merit Based Immigration. Go for it! WIN! 15 Jun 2018 17:08

It is the Democrats fault for being weak and ineffective with Boarder Security and Crime. Tell them to start thinking about the people devastated by Crime coming from illegal immigration. Change the laws! 18 Jun 2018 13:53

I want to take a moment to address the current illegal immigration crisis on the Southern Border...it has been going on for many many decades... 19 Jun 2018 18:04

The Fake News is not mentioning the safety and security of our Country when talking about illegal immigration. Our immigration laws are the weakest and worst anywhere in the world and the Dems will do anything not to change them & to obstruct-want open borders which means crime! 20 Jun 2018 12:25

We shouldn't be hiring judges by the thousands as our ridiculous immigration laws demand we should be changing our laws building the Wall hire Border Agents and Ice and not let people come into our country based on the legal phrase they are told to say as their password. 21 Jun 2018 12:12

My Administration is acting swiftly to address the illegal immigration crisis on the Southern Border. Loopholes in our immigration laws all supported by extremist open border Democrats...and that's what they are - they're extremist open border Democrats.... 21 Jun 2018 17:02

We are gathered today to hear directly from the AMERICAN VICTIMS of ILLEGAL IMMIGRATION. These are the American Citizens permanently separated from their loved ones b/c they were killed by criminal illegal aliens. These are the families the media ignores... 22 Jun 2018 19:40

RT @realDonaldTrump: We are gathered today to hear directly from the AMERICAN VICTIMS of ILLEGAL IMMIGRATION. These are the American Citize... 23 Jun 2018 11:19

....If this is done illegal immigration will be stopped in it's tracks - and at very little by comparison cost. This is the only real answer - and we must continue to BUILD THE WALL! 25 Jun 2018 12:54

Congressman Matt Gaetz of Florida is one of the finest and most talented people in Congress. Strong on Crime the Border Illegal Immigration the 2nd Amendment our great Military & Vets Matt worked tirelessly on helping to get our Massive Tax Cuts. He has my Full Endorsement! 13 Jul 2018 6:02

Brian Kemp is running for Governor of the great state of Georgia. The Primary is on Tuesday. Brian is tough on crime strong on the border and illegal immigration. He loves our Military and our Vets and protects our Second Amendment. I give him my full and total endorsement. 18 Jul 2018 19:25

I would be willing to "shut down" government if the Democrats do not give us the votes for Border Security which includes the Wall! Must get rid of Lottery Catch & Release etc. and finally go to system of Immigration based on MERIT! We need great people coming into our Country! 29 Jul 2018 13:13

We must have Border Security get rid of Chain Lottery Catch & Release Sanctuary Cities - go to Merit based Immigration. Protect ICE and Law Enforcement and of course keep building but much faster THE WALL! 30 Jul 2018 11:57

Illegal immigration is a top National Security problem. After decades of playing games with the whole World laughing at the stupidity of our immigration laws and with Democrats thinking... 30 Jul 2018 22:34

.@cindyhydesmith has helped me put America First! She's

strong on the Wall is helping me create Jobs loves our Vets and fights for our conservative judges... 23 Aug 2018 21:10

"The record is quite remarkable. The President has faithfully followed the agenda he campaigned on in 2016. People should focus on the results and they're extraordinary!" James Freeman - Wall Street Journal 6 Sep 2018 14:09

When will Republican leadership learn that they are being played like a fiddle by the Democrats on Border Security and Building the Wall? Without Borders we don't have a country. With Open Borders which the Democrats want we have nothing but crime! Finish the Wall! 15 Sep 2018 22:38

I want to know where is the money for Border Security and the WALL in this ridiculous Spending Bill and where will it come from after the Midterms? Dems are obstructing Law Enforcement and Border Security. REPUBLICANS MUST FINALLY GET TOUGH! 20 Sep 2018 11:43

The United States has strongly informed the President of Honduras that if the large Caravan of people heading to the U.S. is not stopped and brought back to Honduras no more money or aid will be given to Honduras effective immediately! 16 Oct 2018 13:05

Hard to believe that with thousands of people from South of the Border walking unimpeded toward our country in the form of large Caravans that the Democrats won't approve legislation that will allow laws for the protection of our country. Great Midterm issue for Republicans! 17 Oct 2018 13:45

The Caravans are a disgrace to the Democrat Party. Change the immigration laws NOW! 21 Oct 2018 19:14

"Shock report: US paying more for illegal immigrant births than Trump's wall"   22 Oct 2018 17:52

Sadly it looks like Mexico's Police and Military are unable to stop the Caravan heading to the Southern Border of the United States. Criminals and unknown Middle Easterners are mixed in. I have alerted Border Patrol and Military that this is a National Emergy. Must change laws! 22 Oct 2018 12:37

Every time you see a Caravan or people illegally coming or attempting to come into our Country illegally think of and blame the Democrats for not giving us the votes to change our pathetic Immigration Laws! Remember the Midterms! So unfair to those who come in legally. 22 Oct 2018 12:49

For those who want and advocate for illegal immigration just take a good look at what has happened to Europe over the last 5 years. A total mess! They only wish they had that decision to make over again. 24 Oct 2018 11:52

Just spoke with Prime Minister @GiuseppeConteIT of Italy concerning many subjects including the fact that Italy is now taking a very hard line on illegal immigration... 25 Oct 2018 18:47

...I agree with their stance 100% and the United States is likewise taking a very hard line on illegal immigration. The Prime Minister is working very hard on the economy of Italy - he will be successful! 25 Oct 2018 18:47

To those in the Caravan turnaround we are not letting people into the United States illegally. Go back to your Country and if you want apply for citizenship like millions of others are doing! 25 Oct 2018 18:31

The United States has been spending Billions of Dollars a year on Illegal Immigration. This will not continue. Democrats must give us the votes to pass strong (but fair) laws. If not we will be forced to play a much tougher hand. 26 Oct 2018 13:55

Many Gang Members and some very bad people are mixed into the Caravan heading to our Southern Border. Please go back you will not be admitted into the United States unless you go through the legal process. This is an invasion of our Country and our Military is waiting for you! 29 Oct 2018 14:41

The Caravans are made up of some very tough fighters and people. Fought back hard and viciously against Mexico at Northern Border before breaking through. Mexican soldiers hurt were unable or unwilling to stop Caravan. Should stop them before they reach our Border but won't! 31 Oct 2018 12:38

Our military is being mobilized at the Southern Border. Many more troops coming. We will NOT let these Caravans which are also made up of some very bad thugs and gang members into the U.S. Our Border is sacred must come in legally. TURN AROUND! 31 Oct 2018 12:45

Illegal immigration affects the lives of all Americans. Illegal

Immigration hurts American workers burdens American taxpayers undermines public safety and places enormous strain on local schools hospitals and communities... 1 Nov 2018 20:54

RT @realDonaldTrump: Illegal immigration affects the lives of all Americans. Illegal Immigration hurts American workers burdens American t... 4 Nov 2018 15:28

Isn't it ironic that large Caravans of people are marching to our border wanting U.S.A. asylum because they are fearful of being in their country - yet they are proudly waving.... 17 Nov 2018 0:43

Catch and Release is an obsolete term. It is now Catch and Detain. Illegal Immigrants trying to come into the U.S.A. often proudly flying the flag of their nation as they ask for U.S. Asylum will be detained or turned away. Dems must approve Border Security & Wall NOW! 18 Nov 2018 19:55

There are a lot of CRIMINALS in the Caravan. We will stop them. Catch and Detain! Judicial Activism by people who know nothing about security and the safety of our citizens is putting our country in great danger. Not good! 21 Nov 2018 21:42

Republicans and Democrats MUST come together finally with a major Border Security package which will include funding for the Wall. After 40 years of talk it is finally time for action. Fix the Border for once and for all NOW! 23 Nov 2018 12:41

Would be very SMART if Mexico would stop the Caravans long before they get to our Southern Border or if originating countries would not let them form (it is a way they get certain people out of their country and dump in U.S. No longer). Dems created this problem. No crossings! 25 Nov 2018 13:28

Mexico should move the flag waving Migrants many of whom are stone cold criminals back to their countries. Do it by plane do it by bus do it anyway you want but they are NOT coming into the U.S.A. We will close the Border permanently if need be. Congress fund the WALL! 26 Nov 2018 11:19

We would save Billions of Dollars if the Democrats would give us the votes to build the Wall. Either way people will NOT be allowed into our Country illegally! We will close the entire Southern Border if necessary. Also STOP THE DRUGS! 3 Dec 2018 13:45

Could somebody please explain to the Democrats (we need their votes) that our Country losses 250 Billion Dollars a year on illegal immigration not including the terrible drug flow. Top Border Security including a Wall is $25 Billion. Pays for itself in two months. Get it done! 4 Dec 2018 16:22

Arizona together with our Military and Border Patrol is bracing for a massive surge at a NON-WALLED area. WE WILL NOT LET THEM THROUGH. Big danger. Nancy and Chuck must approve Boarder Security and the Wall! 7 Dec 2018 3:15

Despite the large Caravans that WERE forming and heading to our Country people have not been able to get through our newly built Walls makeshift Walls & Fences or Border Patrol Officers & Military. They are now staying in Mexico or going back to their original countries....... 11 Dec 2018 11:52

.....Ice Border Patrol and our Military have done a FANTASTIC job of securing our Southern Border. A Great Wall would be however a far easier & less expensive solution. We have already built large new sections & fully renovated others making them like new. The Democrats..... 11 Dec 2018 12:04

.....I look forward to my meeting with Chuck Schumer & Nancy Pelosi. In 2006 Democrats voted for a Wall and they were right to do so. Today they no longer want Border Security. They will fight it at all cost and Nancy must get votes for Speaker. But the Wall will get built... 11 Dec 2018 12:30

....People do not yet realize how much of the Wall including really effective renovation has already been built. If the Democrats do not give us the votes to secure our Country the Military will build the remaining sections of the Wall. They know how important it is! 11 Dec 2018 12:42

The Democrats and President Obama gave Iran 150 Billion Dollars and got nothing but they can't give 5 Billion Dollars for National Security and a Wall? 12 Dec 2018 12:50

I often stated "One way or the other Mexico is going to pay for the Wall." This has never changed. Our new deal with Mexico (and Canada) the USMCA is so much better than the old very costly & anti-USA NAFTA deal that just by the money we save MEXICO IS PAYING FOR THE WALL! 13 Dec 2018 12:38

Anytime you hear a Democrat saying that you can have good Border Security without a Wall write them off as just another politician following the party line. Time for us to save billions of dollars a year and have at the same time far greater safety and control! 17 Dec 2018 16:05

Illegal immigration costs the United States more than 200 Billion Dollars a year. How was this allowed to happen? 18 Dec 2018 12:55

The Democrats are saying loud and clear that they do not want to build a Concrete Wall - but we are not building a Concrete Wall we are building artistically designed steel slats so that you can easily see through it.... 19 Dec 2018 1:13

In our Country so much money has been poured down the drain for so many years but the Democrats fight us like cats and dogs when it comes to spending on Boarder Security (including a Wall) and the Military. We won on the Military it is being completely rebuilt. We will win... 19 Dec 2018 12:28

In our Country so much money has been poured down the drain for so many years but when it comes to Border Security and the Military the Democrats fight to the death. We won on the Military which is being completely rebuilt. One way or the other we will win on the Wall! 19 Dec 2018 12:35

Mexico is paying (indirectly) for the Wall through the new USMCA the replacement for NAFTA! Far more money coming to the U.S. Because of the tremendous dangers at the Border including large scale criminal and drug inflow the United States Military will build the Wall! 19 Dec 2018 13:43

The Democrats who know Steel Slats (Wall) are necessary for Border Security are putting politics over Country. What they are just beginning to realize is that I will not sign any of their legislation including infrastructure unless it has perfect Border Security. U.S.A. WINS! 20 Dec 2018 12:28

With so much talk about the Wall people are losing sight of the great job being done on our Southern Border by Border Patrol ICE and our great Military. Remember the Caravans? Well they didn't get through and none are forming or on their way. Border is tight. Fake News silent! 20 Dec 2018 12:39

When I begrudgingly signed the Omnibus Bill I was promised the Wall and Border Security by leadership. Would be done by end of year (NOW). It didn't happen! We foolishly fight for Border Security for other countries - but not for our beloved U.S.A. Not good! 20 Dec 2018 15:28

Build That Wall

Thank you to our GREAT Republican Members of Congress for your VOTE to fund Border Security and the Wall. The final numbers were 217-185 and many have said that the enthusiasm was greater than they have ever seen before. So proud of you all. Now on to the Senate! 21 Dec 2018 3:13

Senator Mitch McConnell should fight for the Wall and Border Security as hard as he fought for anything. He will need Democrat votes but as shown in the House good things happen. If enough Dems don't vote it will be a Democrat Shutdown! House Republicans were great yesterday! 21 Dec 2018 11:50

The Democrats are trying to belittle the concept of a Wall calling it old fashioned. The fact is there is nothing else's that will work and that has been true for thousands of years. It's like the wheel there is nothing better. I know tech better than anyone & technology..... 21 Dec 2018 11:58

.....on a Border is only effective in conjunction with a Wall. Properly designed and built Walls work and the Democrats are lying when they say they don't. In Israel the Wall is 99.9% successful. Will not be any different on our Southern Border! Hundreds of $Billions saved! 21 Dec 2018 12:10

No matter what happens today in the Senate Republican House Members should be very proud of themselves. They flew back to Washington from all parts of the World in order to vote for Border Security and the Wall. Not one Democrat voted yes and we won big. I am very proud of you! 21 Dec 2018 12:19

The Democrats whose votes we need in the Senate will probably vote against Border Security and the Wall even though they know it is DESPERATELY NEEDED. If the Dems vote no there will be a shutdown that will last for a very long time. People don't want Open Borders and Crime! 21 Dec 2018 12:24

Even President Ronald Reagan tried for 8 years to build a Border Wall or Fence and was unable to do so. Others also have tried. We will get it done one way or the other! 21 Dec 2018 12:38

The crisis of illegal activity at our Southern Border is real and will not stop until we build a great Steel Barrier or Wall. Let work begin! 22 Dec 2018 20:03

The only way to stop drugs gangs human trafficking criminal

elements and much else from coming into our Country is with a Wall or Barrier. Drones and all of the rest are wonderful and lots of fun but it is only a good old fashioned Wall that works! 23 Dec 2018 14:17

The most important way to stop gangs drugs human trafficking and massive crime is at our Southern Border. We need Border Security and as EVERYONE knows you can't have Border Security without a Wall. The Drones & Technology are just bells and whistles. Safety for America! 24 Dec 2018 4:05

Virtually every Democrat we are dealing with today strongly supported a Border Wall or Fence. It was only when I made it an important part of my campaign because people and drugs were pouring into our Country unchecked that they turned against it. Desperately needed! 24 Dec 2018 14:31

The Wall is different than the 25 Billion Dollars in Border Security. The complete Wall will be built with the Shutdown money plus funds already in hand. The reporting has been inaccurate on the point. The problem is without the Wall much of the rest of Dollars are wasted! 24 Dec 2018 17:10

I am all alone (poor me) in the White House waiting for the Democrats to come back and make a deal on desperately needed Border Security. At some point the Democrats not wanting to make a deal will cost our Country more money than the Border Wall we are all talking about. Crazy! 24 Dec 2018 17:32

I am in the Oval Office & just gave out a 115 mile long contract for another large section of the Wall in Texas. We are already building and renovating many miles of Wall some complete. Democrats must end Shutdown and finish funding. Billions of Dollars & lives will be saved! 24 Dec 2018 22:24

Have the Democrats finally realized that we desperately need Border Security and a Wall on the Southern Border. Need to stop Drugs Human TraffickingGang Members & Criminals from coming into our Country. Do the Dems realize that most of the people not getting paid are Democrats? 27 Dec 2018 12:06

The reason the DACA for Wall deal didn't get done was that a ridiculous court decision from the 9th Circuit allowed DACA to remain thereby setting up a Supteme Court case. After ruling Dems dropped deal - and that's where we are today

Democrat obstruction of the needed Wall. 27 Dec 2018 19:35

The Democrats OBSTRUCTION of the desperately needed Wall where they almost all recently agreed it should be built is exceeded only by their OBSTRUCTION of 350 great people wanting & expecting to come into Government after being delayed for more than two years a U.S. record! 27 Dec 2018 19:41

The reason the DACA for Wall deal didn't get done was that a ridiculous court decision from the 9th Circuit allowed DACA to remain thereby setting up a Supreme Court case. After ruling Dems dropped deal - and that's where we are today Democrat obstruction of the needed Wall. 27 Dec 2018 19:44

"Border Patrol Agents want the Wall." Democrat's say they don't want the Wall (even though they know it is really needed) and they don't want ICE. They don't have much to campaign on do they? An Open Southern Border and the large scale crime that comes with such stupidity! 27 Dec 2018 20:39

There is right now a full scale manhunt going on in California for an illegal immigrant accused of shooting and killing a police officer during a traffic stop. Time to get tough on Border Security. Build the Wall! 27 Dec 2018 21:04

This isn't about the Wall everybody knows that a Wall will work perfectly (In Israel the Wall works 99.9%). This is only about the Dems not letting Donald Trump & the Republicans have a win. They may have the 10 Senate votes but we have the issue Border Security. 2020! 27 Dec 2018 22:10

We will be forced to close the Southern Border entirely if the Obstructionist Democrats do not give us the money to finish the Wall & also change the ridiculous immigration laws that our Country is saddled with. Hard to believe there was a Congress & President who would approve! 28 Dec 2018 12:16

....The United States looses soooo much money on Trade with Mexico under NAFTA over 75 Billion Dollars a year (not including Drug Money which would be many times that amount) that I would consider closing the Southern Border a "profit making operation." We build a Wall or..... 28 Dec 2018 12:42

.....close the Southern Border. Bring our car industry back into the United States where it belongs. Go back to pre-NAFTA before so many of our companies and jobs were so foolishly sent to Mexico. Either we build (finish) the Wall or we close the Border...... 28 Dec 2018 12:49

.....Honduras, Guatemala and El Salvador are doing nothing for the United States but taking our money. Word is that a new Caravan is forming in Honduras and they are doing nothing about it. We will be cutting off all aid to these 3 countries - taking advantage of U.S. for years! 28 Dec 2018 13:06

Any deaths of children or others at the Border are strictly the fault of the Democrats and their pathetic immigration policies that allow people to make the long trek thinking they can enter our country illegally. They can't. If we had a Wall they wouldn't even try! The two..... 29 Dec 2018 18:30

...children in question were very sick before they were given over to Border Patrol. The father of the young girl said it was not their fault he hadn't given her water in days. Border Patrol needs the Wall and it will all end. They are working so hard & getting so little credit! 29 Dec 2018 18:36

For those that naively ask why didn't the Republicans get approval to build the Wall over the last year it is because IN THE SENATE WE NEED 10 DEMOCRAT VOTES and they will gives us "NONE" for Border Security! Now we have to do it the hard way with a Shutdown. Too bad! @FoxNews 29 Dec 2018 19:25

"Absolutely nothing" (on Russian Collusion). Kimberley Strassel The Wall Street Journal. The Russian Collusion fabrication is the greatest Hoax in the history of American politics. The only Russian Collusion was with Hillary and the Democrats! 30 Dec 2018 3:01

President and Mrs. Obama built/has a ten foot Wall around their D.C. mansion/compound. I agree totally necessary for their safety and security. The U.S. needs the same thing slightly larger version! 30 Dec 2018 21:59

An all concrete Wall was NEVER ABANDONED as has been reported by the media. Some areas will be all concrete but the experts at Border Patrol prefer a Wall that is see through (thereby making it possible to see what is happening on both sides). Makes sense to me! 31 Dec 2018 12:51

I campaigned on Border Security which you cannot have without a strong and powerful Wall. Our Southern Border has long been an "Open Wound" where drugs criminals (including human traffickers) and illegals would pour into our Country. Dems should get back here an fix now! 31 Dec 2018 13:29

I'm in the Oval Office. Democrats come back from vacation now and give us the votes necessary for Border Security including the Wall. You voted yes in 2006 and 3013. One more yes but with me in office I'll get it built and Fast! 31 Dec 2018 15:33

I'm in the Oval Office. Democrats come back from vacation now and give us the votes necessary for Border Security including the Wall. You voted yes in 2006 and 2013. One more yes but with me in office I'll get it built and Fast! 31 Dec 2018 15:37

It's incredible how Democrats can all use their ridiculous sound bite and say that a Wall doesn't work. It does and properly built almost 100%! They say it's old technology - but so is the wheel. They now say it is immoral- but it is far more immoral for people to be dying! 31 Dec 2018 15:39

Radical Islamic Terrorism

Libya is being taken over by Islamic radicals---with @BarackObama's open support. 31 Aug 2011 16:07

The US Air Force won the war in Libya to clear the way for Islamic Extremist control of Libya. 27 Oct 2011 19:37

The Arab Spring has turned into the Islamist Winter. Our ally @Israel is in a perilous position. We must stand behind @Israel. 11 Nov 2011 19:31

Egypt is turning into a hot bed of radical Islam. The current protest is another coup attempt. We should never have abandoned Mubarak. 21 Nov 2011 21:58

Why does @BarackObama support the radical Islamists in Egypt protests yet has such a high disregard for the Tea Party? 28 Nov 2011 19:44

A clip of my upcoming interview with @DavidBrody discussing #TimeToGetTough @Israel and the Islamist winter 8 Dec 2011 18:45

Why does @BarackObama continue to defend radical Islam? He is calling the Ft. Hood massacre "workplace violence." 8 Dec 2011 20:46

The Islamists are taking over Egypt through the election. Why did @BarackObama force Mubarak out? He was an ally. 30 Jan 2012 20:39

@BarackObama's budget funds the "Arab Spring" with $800B and the Muslim Brotherhood in Egypt $1.3B in military aid. He loves radical Islam. 14 Feb 2012 19:45

Welcome to the 'Islamist Winter' - the Muslim Brotherhood is now taking over the Egyptian military and possibly (cont) 28 Mar 2012 19:02

THe WH should not have hosted the Muslim Brotherhood. @BarackObama's friends are enemies of the US and @Israel. The Islamist winter is here. 6 Apr 2012 17:23

The Islamists have won. Just as I predicted the Muslim Brotherhood has taken over Egypt. @BarackObama never should have abandoned Mubarek. 25 Jun 2012 17:31

It's Wednesday how many more of our embassies will be stormed by Islamists? 12 Sep 2012 19:08

Now every time Islamic militants attack they will use that movie as an excuse. What was the excuse before the movie? 20 Sep 2012 19:02

Obama wants to unilaterally put a no-fly zone in Syria to protect Al Qaeda Islamists as Syria is NOT our problem. 29 May 2013 18:58

Obama believes Benghazi is a "phony scandal." Nothing phony about Americans being killed by Islamists. 31 Jul 2013 19:56

Many of the Syrian rebels are radical jihadi Islamists who are murdering Christians. Why would we ever fight with them? 6 Sep 2013 18:44

These Islamists chop Americans' heads off and want to destroy us. We should be applauding the CIA not persecuting them. 11 Dec 2014 21:51

Obama attacks the CIA for waterboarding while routinely droning civilians caught in the Islamist crosshairs. 16 Dec 2014 20:45

@lancebagley1: Great Article DonaldTrump   ISIS in competition w/ Trump #MakeAmericaGreatAgain & Kill Islambies!!! 19 May 2015 2:18

@AlbertoZambrano: @HeinzFGuderian   Well get your facts straight. McCain was so bad he gave us Obama. He gave arms to Islamic terrorists 21 Jul 2015 5:38

@shawnlivinlife: I still haven't heard the WH say the words islamic terrorist. Call it what it is. #Trump2016 can't happen fast enough. 14 Nov 2015 23:30

Why won't President Obama use the term Islamic Terrorism? Isn't it now after all of this time and so much death about time! 15 Nov 2015 3:30

When will President Obama issue the words RADICAL ISLAMIC TERRORISM? He can't say it and unless he will the problem will not be solved! 15 Nov 2015 14:18

I didn't suggest a database-a reporter did. We must defeat Islamic terrorism & have surveillance including a watch list to protect America 20 Nov 2015 18:51

We better get tough with RADICAL ISLAMIC TERRORISTS and get tough now or the life and safety of our wonderful country will be in jeopardy! 22 Nov 2015 15:59

Wonder if Obama will ever say RADICAL ISLAMIC TERRORIST? 6 Dec 2015 0:42

Hillary just said that she will not use the term "radical Islamic" - but was incapable of saying why. She is afraid of Obama & the e-mails! 6 Dec 2015 15:25

BIG NIGHT ON TWITTER TONIGHT. I WILL BE LIVE TWEETING PRESIDENT OBAMA'S SPEECH AT 7:50 P.M. (EASTERN). MUST TALK RADICAL ISLAMIC TERRORISM! 7 Dec 2015 0:27

Hillary won't call out radical Islam! She will be soundly defeated. 7 Dec 2015 0:55

Well Obama refused to say (he just can't say it) that we are at WAR with RADICAL ISLAMIC TERRORISTS. 7 Dec 2015 1:45

Our country is facing a major threat from radical Islamic terrorism. We better get very smart and very tough FAST before it is too late! 9 Dec 2015 2:56

More radical Islam attacks today - it never ends! Strengthen the borders we must be vigilant and smart. No more being politically correct. 16 Jan 2016 2:47

Far more killed than anticipated in radical Islamic terror attack yesterday. Get tough and smart U.S. or we won't have a country anymore! 17 Jan 2016 20:57

Boycott all Apple products until such time as Apple gives cellphone info to authorities regarding radical Islamic terrorist couple from Cal 19 Feb 2016 21:38

Another radical Islamic attack this time in Pakistan targeting Christian women & children. At least 67 dead400 injured. I alone can solve 27 Mar 2016 20:37

Appreciate the congrats for being right on radical Islamic terrorism I don't want congrats I want toughness & vigilance. We must be smart! 12 Jun 2016 16:43

Is President Obama going to finally mention the words radical Islamic terrorism? If he doesn't he should immediately resign in disgrace! 12 Jun 2016 17:58

In my speech on protecting America I spoke about a temporary ban which includes suspending immigration from nations tied to Islamic terror. 13 Jun 2016 21:10

With Hillary and Obama the terrorist attacks will only get worse. Politically correct fools won't even call it what it is - RADICAL ISLAM! 4 Jul 2016 15:34

I highly recommend the just out book - THE FIELD OF FIGHT - by General Michael Flynn. How to defeat radical Islam. 23 Jul 2016 3:49

Hillary's refusal to mention Radical Islam as she pushes a 550% increase in refugees is more proof that she is unfit to lead the country. 29 Jul 2016 3:47

Our way of life is under threat by Radical Islam and Hillary Clinton cannot even bring herself to say the words. 29 Jul 2016 3:50

Captain Khan killed 12 years ago was a hero but this is about RADICAL ISLAMIC TERROR and the weakness of our "leaders" to eradicate it! 31 Jul 2016 12:57

This story is not about Mr. Khan who is all over the place doing interviews but rather RADICAL ISLAMIC TERRORISM and the U.S. Get smart! 1 Aug 2016 11:27

Hillary Clinton raked in money from regimes that horribly oppress women and gays & refuses to speak out against Radical Islam. 1 Aug 2016 22:52

Our thoughts are with the forces fighting ISIS in Iraq. We must never back down against this extreme radical Islami... 17 Oct 2016 17:50

Thank you Colorado Springs. If I'm elected President I am going to keep Radical Islamic Terrorists out of our count... 18 Oct 2016 19:53

Hillary has called for 550% more Syrian immigrants but won't even mention "radical Islamic terrorists." #Debate... 20 Oct 2016 1:34

If elected POTUS - I will stop RADICAL ISLAMIC TERRORISM in this country! In order to do this we need to... 20 Oct 2016 15:52

Thank you Geneva Ohio. If I am elected President I am going to keep RADICAL ISLAMIC TERRORISTS OUT of our countr... 28 Oct 2016 1:47

A new radical Islamic terrorist has just attacked in Louvre Museum in Paris. Tourists were locked down. France on edge again. GET SMART U.S. 3 Feb 2017 12:51

The threat from radical Islamic terrorism is very real just look at what is happening in Europe and the Middle-East. Courts must act fast! 7 Feb 2017 2:49

Study what General Pershing of the United States did to terrorists when caught. There was no more Radical Islamic Terror for 35 years! 17 Aug 2017 18:45

Radical Islamic Terrorism must be stopped by whatever means necessary! The courts must give us back our protective rights. Have to be tough! 18 Aug 2017 13:06

Just out report: "United Kingdom crime rises 13% annually amid spread of Radical Islamic terror." Not good we must keep America safe! 20 Oct 2017 10:31

RT @JaydaBF: VIDEO: Islamist mob pushes teenage boy off roof and beats him to death! 29 Nov 2017 11:44

Theresa @theresamay don't focus on me focus on the destructive Radical Islamic Terrorism that is taking place within the United Kingdom. We are doing just fine! 30 Nov 2017 0:43

.@Theresa_May don't focus on me focus on the destructive Radical Islamic Terrorism that is taking place within the United Kingdom. We are doing just fine! 30 Nov 2017 1:02

France honors a great hero. Officer died after bravely swapping places with hostage in ISIS related terror attack. So much bravery around the world constantly fighting radical Islamic terrorism. Even stronger measures needed especially at borders! 25 Mar 2018 10:10

Enemy of the People

Reports by @CNN that I will be working on The Apprentice during my Presidency even part time are ridiculous & untrue - FAKE NEWS! 10 Dec 2016 14:11

FAKE NEWS - A TOTAL POLITICAL WITCH HUNT! 11 Jan 2017 1:19

I win an election easily a great "movement" is verified and crooked opponents try to belittle our victory with FAKE NEWS. A sorry state! 11 Jan 2017 12:44

Intelligence agencies should never have allowed this fake news to "leak" into the public. One last shot at me.Are we living in Nazi Germany? 11 Jan 2017 12:48

We had a great News Conference at Trump Tower today. A couple of FAKE NEWS organizations were there but the people truly get what's going on 12 Jan 2017 4:01

.@CNN is in a total meltdown with their FAKE NEWS because their ratings are tanking since election and their credibility will soon be gone! 12 Jan 2017 14:22

Totally made up facts by sleazebag political operatives both Democrats and Republicans - FAKE NEWS! Russia says nothing exists. Probably... 13 Jan 2017 11:11

much worse - just look at Syria (red line) Crimea Ukraine and the build-up of Russian nukes. Not good! Was this the leaker of Fake News? 16 Jan 2017 0:29

to the U.S. but had nothing to do with TRUMP is more FAKE NEWS. Ask top CEO's of those companies for real facts. Came back because of me! 18 Jan 2017 12:44

Congratulations to @FoxNews for being number one in inauguration ratings. They were many times higher than FAKE NEWS @CNN - public is smart! 25 Jan 2017 2:16

The failing @nytimes has been wrong about me from the very beginning. Said I would lose the primaries then the general election. FAKE NEWS! 28 Jan 2017 13:04

Somebody with aptitude and conviction should buy the FAKE NEWS and failing @nytimes and either run it correctly or let it fold with dignity! 29 Jan 2017 13:00

Thank you to Prime Minister of Australia for telling the truth about our very civil conversation that FAKE NEWS media lied about. Very nice! 3 Feb 2017 11:34

After being forced to apologize for its bad and inaccurate coverage of me after winning the election the FAKE NEWS @nytimes is still lost! 4 Feb 2017 13:39

Any negative polls are fake news just like the CNN ABC NBC polls in the election. Sorry people want border security and extreme vetting. 6 Feb 2017 12:01

I call my own shots largely based on an accumulation of data and everyone knows it. Some FAKE NEWS media in order to marginalize lies! 6 Feb 2017 12:07

16 Fake News Stories Reporters Have Run Since Trump Won' 8 Feb 2017 15:54

Chris Cuomo in his interview with Sen. Blumenthal never asked him about his long-term lie about his brave "service" in Vietnam. FAKE NEWS! 9 Feb 2017 13:19

The failing @nytimes does major FAKE NEWS China story saying "Mr.Xi has not spoken to Mr. Trump since Nov.14." We spoke at length yesterday! 10 Feb 2017 13:35

While on FAKE NEWS @CNN Bernie Sanders was cut off for using the term fake news to describe the network. They said technical difficulties! 12 Feb 2017 12:14

Just leaving Florida. Big crowds of enthusiastic supporters lining the road that the FAKE NEWS media refuses to mention. Very dishonest! 12 Feb 2017 22:19

The fake news media is going crazy with their conspiracy theories and blind hatred. @MSNBC & @CNN are unwatchable. @foxandfriends is great! 15 Feb 2017 11:40

FAKE NEWS media which makes up stories and "sources" is far more effective than the discredited Democrats - but they are fading fast! 16 Feb 2017 14:10

The Democrats had to come up with a story as to why they lost the election and so badly (306) so they made up a story - RUSSIA. Fake news! 16 Feb 2017 14:39

The FAKE NEWS media (failing @nytimes @CNN @NBCNews and many more) is not my enemy it is the enemy of the American people. SICK! 17 Feb 2017 21:32

The FAKE NEWS media (failing @nytimes @NBCNews @ABC @CBS @CNN) is not my enemy it is the enemy of the American People! 17 Feb 2017 21:48

Don't believe the main stream (fake news) media.The White House is running VERY WELL. I inherited a MESS and am in the process of fixing it. 18 Feb 2017 13:31

Give the public a break - The FAKE NEWS media is trying to say that large scale immigration in Sweden is working out just beautifully. NOT! 20 Feb 2017 14:15

FAKE NEWS media knowingly doesn't tell the truth. A great danger to our country. The failing @nytimes has become a joke. Likewise @CNN. Sad! 25 Feb 2017 3:09

Russia talk is FAKE NEWS put out by the Dems and played up by the media in order to mask the big election defeat and the illegal leaks! 26 Feb 2017 18:16

Don't let the FAKE NEWS tell you that there is big infighting in the Trump Admin. We are getting along great and getting major things done! 7 Mar 2017 14:14

Does anybody really believe that a reporter who nobody ever heard of "went to his mailbox" and found my tax returns? @NBCNews FAKE NEWS! 15 Mar 2017 10:55

Despite what you have heard from the FAKE NEWS I had a GREAT meeting with German Chancellor Angela Merkel. Nevertheless Germany owes..... 18 Mar 2017 13:15

James Clapper and others stated that there is no evidence Potus colluded with Russia. This story is FAKE NEWS and everyone knows it! 20 Mar 2017 10:35

Just heard Fake News CNN is doing polls again despite the fact that their election polls were a WAY OFF disaster. Much higher ratings at Fox 20 Mar 2017 12:35

Just watched the totally biased and fake news reports of the so-called Russia story on NBC and ABC. Such dishonesty! 23 Mar 2017 12:18

Why doesn't Fake News talk about Podesta ties to Russia as covered by @FoxNews or money from Russia to Clinton - sale of Uranium? 28 Mar 2017 22:41

It is the same Fake News Media that said there is "no path to victory for Trump" that is now pushing the phony Russia story. A total scam! 1 Apr 2017 13:02

Anybody (especially Fake News media) who thinks that Repeal & Replace of ObamaCare is dead does not know the love and strength in R Party! 2 Apr 2017 12:56

The two fake news polls released yesterday ABC & NBC while containing some very positive info were totally wrong in General E. Watch! 24 Apr 2017 12:15

The Fake News media is officially out of control. They will do or say anything in order to get attention - never been a time like this! 4 May 2017 11:02

Wowthe Fake News media did everything in its power to make the Republican Healthcare victory look as bad as possible.Far better than Ocare! 5 May 2017 23:22

Why is it that the Fake News rarely reports Ocare is on its last legs and that insurance companies are fleeing for their lives? It's dead! 5 May 2017 23:29

General Flynn was given the highest security clearance by the Obama Administration - but the Fake News seldom likes talking about that. 8 May 2017 11:57

The Roger Stone report on @CNN is false - Fake News. Have not spoken to Roger in a long time - had nothing to do with my decision. 10 May 2017 12:57

Whenever you see the words 'sources say' in the fake news media and they don't mention names.... 28 May 2017 12:34

....it is very possible that those sources don't exsist but are made up by fake news writers. #FakeNews is the enemy! 28 May 2017 12:35

Does anyone notice how the Montana Congressional race was such a big deal to Dems & Fake News until the Republican won? V was poorly covered 28 May 2017 12:40

....it is very possible that those sources don't exist but are made up by fake news writers. #FakeNews is the enemy! 28 May 2017 12:45

Does anyone notice how the Montana Congressional race was such a big deal to Dems & Fake News until the Republican won? V was poorly covered 28 May 2017 12:45

The Fake News Media works hard at disparaging & demeaning my use of social media because they don't want America to hear the real story! 29 May 2017 0:20

Russian officials must be laughing at the U.S. & how a lame excuse for why the Dems lost the election has taken over the Fake News. 30 May 2017 11:04

Sorry folks but if I would have relied on the Fake News of CNN NBC ABC CBS washpost or nytimes I would have had ZERO chance winning WH 6 Jun 2017 12:15

The Fake News Media has never been so wrong or so dirty. Purposely incorrect stories and phony sources to meet their agenda of hate. Sad! 13 Jun 2017 10:35

Fake News is at an all time high. Where is their apology to me for all of the incorrect stories??? 13 Jun 2017 12:48

The Fake News Media hates when I use what has turned out to be my very powerful Social Media - over 100 million people! I can go around them 16 Jun 2017 12:23

Well the Special Elections are over and those that want to MAKE AMERICA GREAT AGAIN are 5 and 0! All the Fake News all the money spent = 0 21 Jun 2017 3:48

Wow CNN had to retract big story on "Russia" with 3 employees forced to resign. What about all the other phony stories they do? FAKE NEWS! 27 Jun 2017 10:33

Fake News CNN is looking at big management changes now that they got caught falsely pushing their phony Russian stories. Ratings way down! 27 Jun 2017 12:30

So they caught Fake News CNN cold but what about NBC CBS & ABC? What about the failing @nytimes & @washingtonpost? They are all Fake News! 27 Jun 2017 12:47

The failing @nytimes writes false story after false story about me. They don't even call to verify the facts of a story. A Fake

News Joke! 28 Jun 2017 10:49

Some of the Fake News Media likes to say that I am not totally engaged in healthcare. Wrong I know the subject well & want victory for U.S. 28 Jun 2017 10:58

The #AmazonWashingtonPost sometimes referred to as the guardian of Amazon not paying internet taxes (which they should) is FAKE NEWS! 28 Jun 2017 13:06

Watched low rated @Morning_Joe for first time in long time. FAKE NEWS. He called me to stop a National Enquirer article. I said no! Bad show 30 Jun 2017 12:55

At some point the Fake News will be forced to discuss our great jobs numbers strong economy success with ISIS the border & so much else! 3 Jul 2017 12:10

Dow hit a new intraday all-time high! I wonder whether or not the Fake News Media will so report? 3 Jul 2017 21:10

I will represent our country well and fight for its interests! Fake News Media will never cover me accurately but who cares! We will #MAGA! 7 Jul 2017 7:44

...have it. Fake News said 17 intel agencies when actually 4 (had to apologize). Why did Obama do NOTHING when he had info before election? 9 Jul 2017 12:06

If Chelsea Clinton were asked to hold the seat for her motheras her mother gave our country away the Fake News would say CHELSEA FOR PRES! 10 Jul 2017 11:47

HillaryClinton can illegally get the questions to the Debate & delete 33000 emails but my son Don is being scorned by the Fake News Media? 16 Jul 2017 10:35

With all of its phony unnamed sources & highly slanted & even fraudulent reporting #Fake News is DISTORTING DEMOCRACY in our country! 16 Jul 2017 11:15

Fake News story of secret dinner with Putin is "sick." All G 20 leaders and spouses were invited by the Chancellor of Germany. Press knew! 19 Jul 2017 0:53

The Fake News is becoming more and more dishonest! Even a dinner arranged for top 20 leaders in Germany is made to look sinister! 19 Jul 2017 0:59

Sean Spicer is a wonderful person who took tremendous abuse from the Fake News Media - but his future is bright! 22 Jul 2017 1:46

While all agree the U. S. President has the complete power to pardon why think of that when only crime so far is LEAKS against us.FAKE NEWS 22 Jul 2017 11:35

Drain the Swamp should be changed to Drain the Sewer - it's actually much worse than anyone ever thought and it begins with the Fake News! 24 Jul 2017 10:40

So many stories about me in the @washingtonpost are Fake News. They are as bad as ratings challenged @CNN. Lobbyist for Amazon and taxes? 25 Jul 2017 2:28

Is Fake News Washington Post being used as a lobbyist weapon against Congress to keep Politicians from looking into Amazon no-tax monopoly? 25 Jul 2017 2:36

...about then candidate Trump." Catherine Herridge @FoxNews. So why doesn't Fake News report this? Witch Hunt! Purposely phony reporting. 27 Jul 2017 13:45

I love reading about all of the "geniuses" who were so instrumental in my election success. Problem is most don't exist. #Fake News! MAGA 29 Jul 2017 23:15

Only the Fake News Media and Trump enemies want me to stop using Social Media (110 million people). Only way for me to get the truth out! 1 Aug 2017 13:55

I love the White House one of the most beautiful buildings (homes) I have ever seen. But Fake News said I called it a dump - TOTALLY UNTRUE 3 Aug 2017 1:29

The Fake News refuses to report the success of the first 6 months: S.C. surging economy & jobsborder & military securityISIS & MS-13 etc. 7 Aug 2017 1:18

The Trump base is far bigger & stronger than ever before (despite some phony Fake News polling). Look at rallies in Penn Iowa Ohio....... 7 Aug 2017 10:58

...and West Virginia. The fact is the Fake News Russian collusion story record Stock Market border security military strength jobs..... 7 Aug 2017 11:04

Hard to believe that with 24/7 #Fake News on CNN ABC NBC

CBS NYTIMES & WAPO the Trump base is getting stronger! 7 Aug 2017 11:18

The Fake News Media will not talk about the importance of the United Nations Security Council's 15-0 vote in favor of sanctions on N. Korea! 7 Aug 2017 20:15

After 200 days rarely has any Administration achieved what we have achieved..not even close! Don't believe the Fake News Suppression Polls! 8 Aug 2017 18:10

Made additional remarks on Charlottesville and realize once again that the #Fake News Media will never be satisfied...truly bad people! 14 Aug 2017 22:29

The public is learning (even more so) how dishonest the Fake News is. They totally misrepresent what I say about hate bigotry etc. Shame! 17 Aug 2017 10:32

Steve Bannon will be a tough and smart new voice at @BreitbartNews...maybe even better than ever before. Fake News needs the competition! 19 Aug 2017 17:47

Heading back to Washington after working hard and watching some of the worst and most dishonest Fake News reporting I have ever seen! 20 Aug 2017 23:22

Jerry Falwell of Liberty University was fantastic on @foxandfriends. The Fake News should listen to what he had to say. Thanks Jerry! 21 Aug 2017 13:27

Thank you the very dishonest Fake News Media is out of control! 21 Aug 2017 13:32

Last night in Phoenix I read the things from my statements on Charlottesville that the Fake News Media didn't cover fairly. People got it! 23 Aug 2017 13:40

The Fake News is now complaining about my different types of back to back speeches. Well their was Afghanistan (somber) the big Rally..... 24 Aug 2017 12:41

The Fake News is now complaining about my different types of back to back speeches. Well there was Afghanistan (somber) the big Rally..... 24 Aug 2017 13:07

General John Kelly is doing a fantastic job as Chief of Staff. There is tremendous spirit and talent in the W.H. Don't believe the Fake News 25 Aug 2017 10:40

Fascinating to watch people writing books and major articles about me and yet they know nothing about me & have zero access. #FAKE NEWS! 12 Sep 2017 12:56

Facebook was always anti-Trump.The Networks were always anti-Trump henceFake News @nytimes(apologized) & @WaPo were anti-Trump. Collusion? 27 Sep 2017 13:36

Fake News CNN and NBC are going out of their way to disparage our great First Responders as a way to "get Trump." Not fair to FR or effort! 30 Sep 2017 11:48

The Fake News Networks are working overtime in Puerto Rico doing their best to take the spirit away from our soldiers and first R's. Shame! 30 Sep 2017 12:07

Despite the Fake News Media in conjunction with the Dems an amazing job is being done in Puerto Rico. Great people! 30 Sep 2017 18:04

In analyzing the Alabama Primary race Fake News always fails to mention that the candidate I endorsed went up MANY points after Election! 30 Sep 2017 23:16

In analyzing the Alabama Primary raceFAKE NEWS always fails to mention that the candidate I endorsed went up MANY points after endorsement! 30 Sep 2017 23:24

We have done a great job with the almost impossible situation in Puerto Rico. Outside of the Fake News or politically motivated ingrates... 1 Oct 2017 12:22

Wow so many Fake News stories today. No matter what I do or say they will not write or speak truth. The Fake News Media is out of control! 4 Oct 2017 11:29

RT @FoxNews: Geraldo Blasts 'Fake News' Reports About Trump's Visit to Puerto Rico 5 Oct 2017 10:30

Why Isn't the Senate Intel Committee looking into the Fake News Networks in OUR country to see why so much of our news is just made up-FAKE! 5 Oct 2017 10:59

Rex Tillerson never threatened to resign. This is Fake News put out by @NBCNews. Low news and reporting standards. No verification from me. 5 Oct 2017 11:50

The Fake News is at it again this time trying to hurt one of the finest people I know General John Kelly by saying he will soon be..... 11 Oct 2017 1:15

It would be really nice if the Fake News Media would report the virtually unprecedented Stock Market growth since the election.Need tax cuts 11 Oct 2017 10:31

With all of the Fake News coming out of NBC and the Networks at what point is it appropriate to challenge their License? Bad for country! 11 Oct 2017 13:55

The Fake News Is going all out in order to demean and denigrate! Such hatred! 12 Oct 2017 12:45

Sadly they and others are Fake News and the public is just beginning to figure it out! 13 Oct 2017 11:10

So much Fake News being put in dying magazines and newspapers. Only place worse may be @NBCNews @CBSNews @ABC and @CNN. Fiction writers! 17 Oct 2017 21:51

The Fake News is going crazy with wacky Congresswoman Wilson(D) who was SECRETLY on a very personal call and gave a total lie on content! 20 Oct 2017 2:53

I hope the Fake News Media keeps talking about Wacky Congresswoman Wilson in that she as a representative is killing the Democrat Party! 21 Oct 2017 12:07

Stock Market hits another all time high on Friday. 5.3 trillion dollars up since Election. Fake News doesn't spent much time on this! 21 Oct 2017 13:14

Keep hearing about "tiny" amount of money spent on Facebook ads. What about the billions of dollars of Fake News on CNN ABC NBC & CBS? 21 Oct 2017 20:06

It is finally sinking through. 46% OF PEOPLE BELIEVE MAJOR NATIONAL NEWS ORGS FABRICATE STORIES ABOUT ME. FAKE NEWS even worse! Lost cred. 22 Oct 2017 12:08

Clinton campaign & DNC paid for research that led to the anti-Trump Fake News Dossier. The victim here is the President. @FoxNews 25 Oct 2017 11:21

Just read the nice remarks by President Jimmy Carter about me and how badly I am treated by the press (Fake News). Thank you Mr. President! 28 Oct 2017 12:28

The Fake News is working overtime. As Paul Manaforts lawyer said there was "no collusion" and events mentioned took place long before he... 31 Oct 2017 12:09

....earth shattering. He and his brother could Drain The Swamp which would be yet another campaign promise fulfilled. Fake News weak! 31 Oct 2017 14:10

The rigged Dem Primary one of the biggest political stories in years got ZERO coverage on Fake News Network TV last night. Disgraceful! 3 Nov 2017 16:09

Wow even I didn't realize we did so much. Wish the Fake News would report! Thank you. 25 Nov 2017 23:25

We should have a contest as to which of the Networks plus CNN and not including Fox is the most dishonest corrupt and/or distorted in its political coverage of your favorite President (me). They are all bad. Winner to receive the FAKE NEWS TROPHY! 27 Nov 2017 14:04

Great and we should boycott Fake News CNN. Dealing with them is a total waste of time! 29 Nov 2017 11:49

Wow Matt Lauer was just fired from NBC for "inappropriate sexual behavior in the workplace." But when will the top executives at NBC & Comcast be fired for putting out so much Fake News. Check out Andy Lack's past! 29 Nov 2017 12:16

So now tha Matt Lauer is gone when will the Fake News practitioners at NBC be terminating the contract of Phil Griffin? And will they terminate low ratings Joe Scarborough based on the "unsolved mystery" that took place in Florida years ago? Investigate! 29 Nov 2017 13:58

So now that Matt Lauer is gone when will the Fake News practitioners at NBC be terminating the contract of Phil Griffin? And will they terminate low ratings Joe Scarborough based on the "unsolved mystery" that took place in Florida years ago? Investigate! 29 Nov 2017 14:14

The media has been speculating that I fired Rex Tillerson or that he would be leaving soon - FAKE NEWS! He's not leaving and while we disagree on certain subjects (I call the final shots) we work well together and America is highly respected again! 1 Dec 2017 20:08

Congratulations to @ABC News for suspending Brian Ross for his horrendously inaccurate and dishonest report on the Russia Russia Russia Witch Hunt. More Networks and "papers" should do the same with their Fake News! 3 Dec 2017 2:22

I never asked Comey to stop investigating Flynn. Just more Fake News covering another Comey lie! 3 Dec 2017 11:15

Fake News CNN made a vicious and purposeful mistake yesterday. They were caught red handed just like lonely Brian Ross at ABC News (who should be immediately fired for his "mistake"). Watch to see if @CNN fires those responsible or was it just gross incompetence? 9 Dec 2017 13:02

CNN'S slogan is CNN THE MOST TRUSTED NAME IN NEWS. Everyone knows this is not true that this could in fact be a fraud on the American Public. There are many outlets that are far more trusted than Fake News CNN. Their slogan should be CNN THE LEAST TRUSTED NAME IN NEWS! 9 Dec 2017 13:21

.@DaveWeigel @WashingtonPost put out a phony photo of an empty arena hours before I arrived @ the venue w/ thousands of people outside on their way in. Real photos now shown as I spoke. Packed house many people unable to get in. Demand apology & retraction from FAKE NEWS WaPo! 9 Dec 2017 22:01

.@daveweigel of the Washington Post just admitted that his picture was a FAKE (fraud?) showing an almost empty arena last night for my speech in Pensacola when in fact he knew the arena was packed (as shown also on T.V.). FAKE NEWS he should be fired. 9 Dec 2017 23:14

Things are going really well for our economy a subject the Fake News spends as little time as possible discussing! Stock Market hit another RECORD HIGH unemployment is now at a 17 year low and companies are coming back into the USA. Really good news and much more to come! 10 Dec 2017 13:30

Very little discussion of all the purposely false and defamatory stories put out this week by the Fake News Media. They are out of control - correct reporting means nothing to them. Major lies written then forced to be withdrawn after they are exposed…a stain on America! 10 Dec 2017 21:18

Another false story this time in the Failing @nytimes that I watch 4-8 hours of television a day - Wrong! Also I seldom if ever watch CNN or MSNBC both of which I consider Fake News. I never watch Don Lemon who I once called the "dumbest man on television!" Bad Reporting. 11 Dec 2017 14:17

Despite thousands of hours wasted and many millions of dollars spent the Democrats have been unable to show any collusion with Russia - so now they are moving on to the false accusations and fabricated stories of women who I don't know and/or have never met. FAKE NEWS! 12 Dec 2017 12:10

Wow more than 90% of Fake News Media coverage of me is negative with numerous forced retractions of untrue stories. Hence my use of Social Media the only way to get the truth out. Much of Mainstream Meadia has become a joke! @foxandfriends 13 Dec 2017 13:02

A story in the @washingtonpost that I was close to "rescinding" the nomination of Justice Gorsuch prior to confirmation is FAKE NEWS. I never even wavered and am very proud of him and the job he is doing as a Justice of the U.S. Supreme Court. The unnamed sources don't exist! 19 Dec 2017 15:07

The Tax Cuts are so large and so meaningful and yet the Fake News is working overtime to follow the lead of their friends the defeated Dems and only demean. This is truly a case where the results will speak for themselves starting very soon. Jobs Jobs Jobs! 20 Dec 2017 14:32

The Massive Tax Cuts which the Fake News Media is desperate to write badly about so as to please their Democrat bosses will soon be kicking in and will speak for themselves. Companies are already making big payments to workers. Dems want to raise taxes hate these big Cuts! 21 Dec 2017 12:24

Was @foxandfriends just named the most influential show in news? You deserve it - three great people! The many Fake News Hate Shows should study your formula for success! 21 Dec 2017 12:45

The Stock Market is setting record after record and unemployment is at a 17 year low. So many things accomplished by the Trump Administration perhaps more than any other President in first year. Sadly will never be reported correctly by the Fake News Media! 23 Dec 2017 22:44

The Fake News refuses to talk about how Big and how Strong our BASE is. They show Fake Polls just like they report Fake News. Despite only negative reporting we are doing well - nobody is going to beat us. MAKE AMERICA GREAT AGAIN! 24 Dec 2017 13:48

The Tax Cut/Reform Bill including Massive Alaska Drilling

and the Repeal of the highly unpopular Individual Mandate brought it all together as to what an incredible year we had. Don't let the Fake News convince you otherwise...and our insider Polls are strong! 24 Dec 2017 20:35

While the Fake News loves to talk about my so-called low approval rating @foxandfriends just showed that my rating on Dec. 28 2017 was approximately the same as President Obama on Dec. 28 2009 which was 47%...and this despite massive negative Trump coverage & Russia hoax! 29 Dec 2017 12:46

I use Social Media not because I like to but because it is the only way to fight a VERY dishonest and unfair "press" now often referred to as Fake News Media. Phony and non-existent "sources" are being used more often than ever. Many stories & reports a pure fiction! 30 Dec 2017 22:36

As our Country rapidly grows stronger and smarter I want to wish all of my friends supporters enemies haters and even the very dishonest Fake News Media a Happy and Healthy New Year. 2018 will be a great year for America! 31 Dec 2017 22:18

So much Fake News is being reported. They don't even try to get it right or correct it when they are wrong. They promote the Fake Book of a mentally deranged author who knowingly writes false information. The Mainstream Media is crazed that WE won the election! 13 Jan 2018 22:08

...and they knew exactly what I said and meant. They just wanted a story. FAKE NEWS! 14 Jan 2018 13:01

RT @realDonaldTrump: So much Fake News is being reported. They don't even try to get it right or correct it when they are wrong. They prom... 14 Jan 2018 13:04

Do you notice the Fake News Mainstream Media never likes covering the great and record setting economic news but rather talks about anything negative or that can be turned into the negative. The Russian Collusion Hoax is dead except as it pertains to the Dems. Public gets it! 16 Jan 2018 14:19

And the FAKE NEWS winners are... 18 Jan 2018 1:00

Even Crazy Jim Acosta of Fake News CNN agrees: "Trump World and WH sources dancing in end zone: Trump wins again...Schumer and Dems caved...gambled and lost." Thank you for your honesty Jim! 23 Jan 2018 11:31

So many positive things going on for the U.S.A. and the Fake News Media just doesn't want to go there. Same negative stories over and over again! No wonder the People no longer trust the media whose approval ratings are correctly at their lowest levels in history!   #MAGA 11 Feb 2018 18:21

Funny how the Fake News Media doesn't want to say that the Russian group was formed in 2014 long before my run for President. Maybe they knew I was going to run even though I didn't know! 17 Feb 2018 19:46

The Fake News Media never fails. Hard to ignore this fact from the Vice President of Facebook Ads Rob Goldman! 17 Feb 2018 20:11

The Fake News of big ratings loser CNN. 18 Feb 2018 13:46

I have been much tougher on Russia than Obama just look at the facts. Total Fake News! 20 Feb 2018 13:38

A woman I don't know and to the best of my knowledge never met is on the FRONT PAGE of the Fake News Washington Post saying I kissed her (for two minutes yet) in the lobby of Trump Tower 12 years ago. Never happened! Who would do this in a public space with live security...... 20 Feb 2018 15:16

Bad ratings @CNN & @MSNBC got scammed when they covered the anti-Trump Russia rally wall-to-wall. They probably knew it was Fake News but because it was a rally against me they pushed it hard anyway. Two really dishonest newscasters but the public is wise! 21 Feb 2018 1:08

I never said "give teachers guns" like was stated on Fake News @CNN & @NBC. What I said was to look at the possibility of giving "concealed guns to gun adept teachers with military or special training experience - only the best. 20% of teachers a lot would now be able to 22 Feb 2018 12:26

"School shooting survivor says he quit @CNN Town Hall after refusing scripted question." @TuckerCarlson. Just like so much of CNN Fake News. That's why their ratings are so bad! MSNBC may be worse. 23 Feb 2018 1:26

The new Fake News narrative is that there is CHAOS in the White House. Wrong! People will always come & go and I want strong dialogue before making a final decision. I still have some people that I want to change (always seeking perfection). There is no Chaos only great Energy! 6 Mar 2018 12:55

The Republicans are 5-0 in recent Congressional races a point which the Fake News Media continuously fails to mention. I backed and campaigned for all of the winners. They give me credit for one. Hopefully Rick Saccone will be another big win on Tuesday. 11 Mar 2018 14:02

Rasmussen and others have my approval ratings at around 50% which is higher than Obama and yet the political pundits love saying my approval ratings are "somewhat low." They know they are lying when they say it. Turn off the show - FAKE NEWS! 11 Mar 2018 15:16

The Fake News is beside themselves that McCabe was caught called out and fired. How many hundreds of thousands of dollars was given to wife's campaign by Crooked H friend Terry M who was also under investigation? How many lies? How many leaks? Comey knew it all and much more! 17 Mar 2018 17:34

I called President Putin of Russia to congratulate him on his election victory (in past Obama called him also). The Fake News Media is crazed because they wanted me to excoriate him. They are wrong! Getting along with Russia (and others) is a good thing not a bad thing....... 21 Mar 2018 18:56

Many lawyers and top law firms want to represent me in the Russia case...don't believe the Fake News narrative that it is hard to find a lawyer who wants to take this on. Fame & fortune will NEVER be turned down by a lawyer though some are conflicted. Problem is that a new...... 25 Mar 2018 11:40

So much Fake News. Never been more voluminous or more inaccurate. But through it all our country is doing great! 26 Mar 2018 12:38

So funny to watch Fake News Networks among the most dishonest groups of people I have ever dealt with criticize Sinclair Broadcasting for being biased. Sinclair is far superior to CNN and even more Fake NBC which is a total joke. 2 Apr 2018 13:28

The Fake News Networks those that knowingly have a sick and biased AGENDA are worried about the competition and quality of Sinclair Broadcast. The "Fakers" at CNN NBC ABC &

CBS have done so much dishonest reporting that they should only be allowed to get awards for fiction! 3 Apr 2018 10:34

The Fake News Washington Post Amazon's "chief lobbyist" has another (of many) phony headlines "Trump Defiant As China Adds Trade Penalties." WRONG! Should read "Trump Defiant as U.S. Adds Trade Penalties Will End Barriers And Massive I.P. Theft." Typically bad reporting! 5 Apr 2018 13:10

Do you believe that the Fake News Media is pushing hard on a story that I am going to replace A.G. Jeff Sessions with EPA Chief Scott Pruitt who is doing a great job but is TOTALLY under siege? Do people really believe this stuff? So much of the media is dishonest and corrupt! 6 Apr 2018 14:46

So much Fake News about what is going on in the White House. Very calm and calculated with a big focus on open and fair trade with China the coming North Korea meeting and of course the vicious gas attack in Syria. Feels great to have Bolton & Larry K on board. I (we) are 11 Apr 2018 10:38

If I wanted to fire Robert Mueller in December as reported by the Failing New York Times I would have fired him. Just more Fake News from a biased newspaper! 12 Apr 2018 10:03

The Syrian raid was so perfectly carried out with such precision that the only way the Fake News Media could demean was by my use of the term "Mission Accomplished." I knew they would seize on this but felt it is such a great Military term it should be brought back. Use often! 15 Apr 2018 12:19

Just hit 50% in the Rasmussen Poll much higher than President Obama at same point. With all of the phony stories and Fake News it's hard to believe! Thank you America we are doing Great Things. 15 Apr 2018 14:44

Rasmussen just came out at 51% Approval despite the Fake News Media. They were one of the three most accurate on Election Day. Just about the most inaccurate were CNN and ABC News/Washington Post and they haven't changed (get new pollsters). Much of the media is a Scam! 17 Apr 2018 17:59

A sketch years later about a nonexistent man. A total con job playing the Fake News Media for Fools (but they know it)! 18 Apr 2018 10:08

Can you believe that despite 93% bad stories from the Fake

News Media (should be getting good stories) today we had just about our highest Poll Numbers including those on Election Day? The American public is wise to the phony an dishonest press. Make America Great Again! 20 Apr 2018 20:25

Sleepy Eyes Chuck Todd of Fake News NBC just stated that we have given up so much in our negotiations with North Korea and they have given up nothing. Wow we haven't given up anything & they have agreed to denuclearization (so great for World) site closure & no more testing! 22 Apr 2018 12:50

"Clapper lied about (fraudulent) Dossier leaks to CNN" @foxandfriends FoxNews He is a lying machine who now works for Fake News CNN. 28 Apr 2018 12:58

The White House Correspondents' Dinner is DEAD as we know it. This was a total disaster and an embarrassment to our great Country and all that it stands for. FAKE NEWS is alive and well and beautifully represented on Saturday night! 30 Apr 2018 12:10

The Fake News is going crazy making up false stories and using only unnamed sources (who don't exist). They are totally unhinged and the great success of this Administration is making them do and say things that even they can't believe they are saying. Truly bad people! 30 Apr 2018 22:49

The White House is running very smoothly despite phony Witch Hunts etc. There is great Energy and unending Stamina both necessary to get things done. We are accomplishing the unthinkable and setting positive records while doing so! Fake News is going "bonkers!" 30 Apr 2018 23:02

NBC NEWS is wrong again! They cite "sources" which are constantly wrong. Problem is like so many others the sources probably don't exist they are fabricated fiction! NBC my former home with the Apprentice is now as bad as Fake News CNN. Sad! 4 May 2018 10:45

The Fake News is working overtime. Just reported that despite the tremendous success we are having with the economy & all things else 91% of the Network News about me is negative (Fake). Why do we work so hard in working with the media when it is corrupt? Take away credentials? 9 May 2018 11:38

The Failing New York Times criticized Secretary of State Pompeo for being AWOL (missing) when in fact he was flying to North Korea. Fake News so bad! 9 May 2018 22:38

Why doesn't the Fake News Media state that the Trump Administration's Anti-Trust Division has been and is opposed to the AT&T purchase of Time Warner in a currently ongoing Trial. Such a disgrace in reporting! 11 May 2018 23:49

The so-called leaks coming out of the White House are a massive over exaggeration put out by the Fake News Media in order to make us look as bad as possible. With that being said leakers are traitors and cowards and we will find out who they are! 14 May 2018 20:46

Can you believe that with all of the made up unsourced stories I get from the Fake News Media together with the $10000000 Russian Witch Hunt (there is no Collusion) I now have my best Poll Numbers in a year. Much of the Media may be corrupt but the People truly get it! 15 May 2018 14:08

Despite the disgusting illegal and unwarranted Witch Hunt we have had the most successful first 17 month Administration in U.S. history - by far! Sorry to the Fake News Media and "Haters" but that's the way it is! 17 May 2018 13:52

Fake News Media had me calling Immigrants or Illegal Immigrants "Animals." Wrong! They were begrudgingly forced to withdraw their stories. I referred to MS 13 Gang Members as "Animals" a big difference - and so true. Fake News got it purposely wrong as usual! 18 May 2018 10:51

Reports are there was indeed at least one FBI representative implanted for political purposes into my campaign for president. It took place very early on and long before the phony Russia Hoax became a "hot" Fake News story. If true - all time biggest political scandal! 18 May 2018 13:50

Real @FoxNews is doing great Fake News CNN is dead! 2 Jun 2018 16:46

There was No Collusion with Russia (except by the Democrats). When will this very expensive Witch Hunt Hoax ever end? So bad for our Country. Is the Special Counsel/Justice Department leaking my lawyers letters to the Fake News Media? Should be looking at Dems corruption instead? 2 Jun 2018 17:31

There was No Collusion with Russia (except by the Democrats). When will this very expensive Witch Hunt Hoax ever end? So bad for our Country. Is the Special Counsel/Justice Department leaking my lawyers letters to the Fake News Media? Should be looking at Dems corruption instead? 2 Jun 2018 17:43

The Fake News Media is desperate to distract from the economy and record setting economic numbers and so they keep talking about the phony Russian Witch Hunt. 4 Jun 2018 20:41

Great night for Republicans! Congratulations to John Cox on a really big number in California. He can win. Even Fake News CNN said the Trump impact was really big much bigger than they ever thought possible. So much for the big Blue Wave it may be a big Red Wave. Working hard! 6 Jun 2018 13:16

The Fake News Media has been so unfair and vicious to my wife and our great First Lady Melania. During her recovery from surgery they reported everything from near death to facelift to left the W.H. (and me) for N.Y. or Virginia to abuse. All Fake she is doing really well! 6 Jun 2018 13:48

...Four reporters spotted Melania in the White House last week walking merrily along to a meeting. They never reported the sighting because it would hurt the sick narrative that she was living in a different part of the world was really ill or whatever. Fake News is really bad! 6 Jun 2018 13:54

Many more Republican voters showed up yesterday than the Fake News thought possible. The political pundits just don't get what is going on out there - or they do get it but refuse to report the facts! Remember Dems are High Tax High Crime easy to beat! 6 Jun 2018 14:04

So funny to watch the Fake News especially NBC and CNN. They are fighting hard to downplay the deal with North Korea. 500 days ago they would have "begged" for this deal-looked like war would break out. Our Country's biggest enemy is the Fake News so easily promulgated by fools! 13 Jun 2018 13:30

So the Democrats make up a phony crime Collusion with the Russians pay a fortune to make the crime sound real illegally leak (Comey) classified information so that a Special Councel will be appointed and then Collude to make this pile of garbage take on life in Fake News! 14 Jun 2018 15:08

I've had to beat 17 very talented people including the Bush Dynasty then I had to beat the Clinton Dynasty and now I have to beat a phony Witch Hunt and all of the dishonest people covered in the IG Report...and never forget the Fake News Media. It never ends! 15 Jun 2018 17:49

I have a great relationship with Angela Merkel of Germany but the Fake News Media only shows the bad photos (implying anger) of negotiating an agreement - where I am asking for things that no other American President would ask for! 15 Jun 2018 22:03

The Fake News Media said that I did not get along with other Leaders at the #G7Summit in Canada. They are once again WRONG! 15 Jun 2018 22:23

Please clear up the Fake News! 17 Jun 2018 11:58

Funny how the Fake News in a coordinated effort with each other likes to say I gave sooo much to North Korea because I "met." That's because that's all they have to disparage! We got so much for peace in the world & more is being added in finals. Even got our hostages/remains! 17 Jun 2018 12:40

Washington Post employees want to go on strike because Bezos isn't paying them enough. I think a really long strike would be a great idea. Employees would get more money and we would get rid of Fake News for an extended period of time! Is @WaPo a registered lobbyist? 17 Jun 2018 13:26

Why was the FBI giving so much information to the Fake News Media. They are not supposed to be doing that and knowing the enemy of the people Fake News they put their own spin on it - truth doesn't matter to them! 18 Jun 2018 0:25

If President Obama (who got nowhere with North Korea and would have had to go to war with many millions of people being killed) had gotten along with North Korea and made the initial steps toward a deal that I have the Fake News would have named him a national hero! 18 Jun 2018 14:57

"FBI texts have revealed anti-Trump Bias." @FoxNews Big News but the Fake News doesn't want to cover. Total corruption - the Witch Hunt has turned out to be a scam! At some point soon the Mainstream Media will have to cover correctly too big a story! 20 Jun 2018 14:00

"I REALLY DON'T CARE DO U?" written on the back of Melania's jacket refers to the Fake News Media. Melania has learned how dishonest they are and she truly no longer cares! 21 Jun 2018 21:51

Such a difference in the media coverage of the same immigration policies between the Obama Administration and ours. Actually we have done a far better job in that our facilities are cleaner and better run than were the facilities under Obama. Fake News is working overtime! 25 Jun 2018 12:36

Many good conversations with North Korea-it is going well! In the meantime no Rocket Launches or Nuclear Testing in 8 months. All of Asia is thrilled. Only the Opposition Party which includes the Fake News is complaining. If not for me we would now be at War with North Korea! 3 Jul 2018 11:16

After having written many best selling books and somewhat priding myself on my ability to write it should be noted that the Fake News constantly likes to pour over my tweets looking for a mistake. I capitalize certain words only for emphasis not b/c they should be capitalized! 3 Jul 2018 21:19

After having written many best selling books and somewhat priding myself on my ability to write it should be noted that the Fake News constantly likes to pore over my tweets looking for a mistake. I capitalize certain words only for emphasis not b/c they should be capitalized! 3 Jul 2018 23:13

The failing NY Times Fake News story today about breast feeding must be called out. The U.S. strongly supports breast feeding but we don't believe women should be denied access to formula. Many women need this option because of malnutrition and poverty. 9 Jul 2018 17:04

So funny! I just checked out Fake News CNN for the first time in a long time (they are dying in the ratings) to see if they covered my takedown yesterday of Jim Acosta (actually a nice guy). They didn't! But they did say I already lost in my meeting with Putin. Fake News...... 14 Jul 2018 11:24

There hasn't been a missile or rocket fired in 9 months in North Korea there have been no nuclear tests and we got back our hostages. Who knows how it will all turn out in the end but why isn't the Fake News talking about these wonderful facts? Because it is FAKE NEWS! 15 Jul 2018 16:11

While I had a great meeting with NATO raising vast amounts of money I had an even better meeting with Vladimir Putin of Russia. Sadly it is not being reported that way - the Fake News is going Crazy! 17 Jul 2018 14:22

The meeting between President Putin and myself was a great

success except in the Fake News Media! 18 Jul 2018 0:21

The Fake News Media is going Crazy! They make up stories without any backup sources or proof. Many of the stories written about me and the good people surrounding me are total fiction. Problem is when you complain you just give them more publicity. But I'll complain anyway! 19 Jul 2018 10:37

The Fake News Media wants so badly to see a major confrontation with Russia even a confrontation that could lead to war. They are pushing so recklessly hard and hate the fact that I'll probably have a good relationship with Putin. We are doing MUCH better than any other country! 19 Jul 2018 10:59

"Trump recognized Russian Meddling MANY TIMES." Thank you to @foxandfriends and @FoxNews for actually showing the clips. The Fake News wants no part of that narrative! Too bad they don't want to focus on all of the ECONOMIC and JOBS records being set. 19 Jul 2018 11:13

The Summit with Russia was a great success except with the real enemy of the people the Fake News Media. I look forward to our second meeting so that we can start implementing some of the many things discussed including stopping terrorism security for Israel nuclear........ 19 Jul 2018 13:24

Will the Dems and Fake News ever learn? This is classic! 19 Jul 2018 18:14

RT @realDonaldTrump: Will the Dems and Fake News ever learn? This is classic! 20 Jul 2018 14:35

RT @realDonaldTrump: The Summit with Russia was a great success except with the real enemy of the people the Fake News Media. I look forw... 20 Jul 2018 14:39

I got severely criticized by the Fake News Media for being too nice to President Putin. In the Old Days they would call it Diplomacy. If I was loud & vicious I would have been criticized for being too tough. Remember when they said I was too tough with Chairman Kim? Hypocrites! 20 Jul 2018 21:50

I had a GREAT meeting with Putin and the Fake News used every bit of their energy to try and disparage it. So bad for our country! 22 Jul 2018 13:15

When you hear the Fake News talking negatively about my

meeting with President Putin and all that I gave up remember I gave up NOTHING we merely talked about future benefits for both countries. Also we got along very well which is a good thing except for the Corrupt Media! 23 Jul 2018 12:25

A Rocket has not been launched by North Korea in 9 months. Likewise no Nuclear Tests. Japan is happy all of Asia is happy. But the Fake News is saying without ever asking me (always anonymous sources) that I am angry because it is not going fast enough. Wrong very happy! 23 Jul 2018 13:06

So sad and unfair that the FCC wouldn't approve the Sinclair Broadcast merger with Tribune. This would have been a great and much needed Conservative voice for and of the People. Liberal Fake News NBC and Comcast gets approved much bigger but not Sinclair. Disgraceful! 25 Jul 2018 0:39

....the only Collusion with Russia was with the Democrats so now they are looking at my Tweets (along with 53 million other people) - the rigged Witch Hunt continues! How stupid and unfair to our Country....And so the Fake News doesn't waste my time with dumb questions NO.... 27 Jul 2018 11:38

Democrats who want Open Borders and care little about Crime are incompetent but they have the Fake News Media almost totally on their side! 27 Jul 2018 22:45

Do you think the Fake News Media will ever report on this tweet from Michael? 29 Jul 2018 11:52

RT @realDonaldTrump: Democrats who want Open Borders and care little about Crime are incompetent but they have the Fake News Media almos... 29 Jul 2018 11:59

Had a very good and interesting meeting at the White House with A.G. Sulzberger Publisher of the New York Times. Spent much time talking about the vast amounts of Fake News being put out by the media & how that Fake News has morphed into phrase "Enemy of the People." Sad! 29 Jul 2018 12:30

The Fake News Media is going CRAZY! They are totally unhinged and in many ways after witnessing first hand the damage they do to so many innocent and decent people I enjoy watching. In 7 years when I am no longer in office their ratings will dry up and they will be gone! 31 Jul 2018 13:34

Wow @foxandfriends is blowing away the competition in the morning ratings. Morning Joe is a dead show with very few people watching and sadly Fake News CNN is also doing poorly. Too much hate and inaccurately reported stories - too predictable! 2 Aug 2018 11:04

They asked my daughter Ivanka whether or not the media is the enemy of the people. She correctly said no. It is the FAKE NEWS which is a large percentage of the media that is the enemy of the people! 2 Aug 2018 20:24

The Fake News hates me saying that they are the Enemy of the People only because they know it's TRUE. I am providing a great service by explaining this to the American People. They purposely cause great division & distrust. They can also cause War! They are very dangerous & sick! 5 Aug 2018 11:38

Fake News reporting a complete fabrication that I am concerned about the meeting my wonderful son Donald had in Trump Tower. This was a meeting to get information on an opponent totally legal and done all the time in politics - and it went nowhere. I did not know about it! 5 Aug 2018 12:35

Too bad a large portion of the Media refuses to report the lies and corruption having to do with the Rigged Witch Hunt - but that is why we call them FAKE NEWS! 5 Aug 2018 12:49

The Republicans have now won 8 out of 9 House Seats yet if you listen to the Fake News Media you would think we are being clobbered. Why can't they play it straight so unfair to the Republican Party and in particular your favorite President! 8 Aug 2018 15:14

While I know it's "not presidential" to take on a lowlife like Omarosa and while I would rather not be doing so this is a modern day form of communication and I know the Fake News Media will be working overtime to make even Wacky Omarosa look legitimate as possible. Sorry! 13 Aug 2018 14:21

....such wonderful and powerful things about me - a true Champion of Civil Rights - until she got fired. Omarosa had Zero credibility with the Media (they didn't want interviews) when she worked in the White House. Now that she says bad about me they will talk to her. Fake News! 14 Aug 2018 1:57

THE FAKE NEWS MEDIA IS THE OPPOSITION PARTY. It is very bad for our Great Country....BUT WE ARE WINNING! 16 Aug 2018 12:50

There is nothing that I would want more for our Country than true FREEDOM OF THE PRESS. The fact is that the Press is FREE to write and say anything it wants but much of what it says is FAKE NEWS pushing a political agenda or just plain trying to hurt people. HONESTY WINS! 16 Aug 2018 14:10

.....Censorship is a very dangerous thing & absolutely impossible to police. If you are weeding out Fake News there is nothing so Fake as CNN & MSNBC & yet I do not ask that their sick behavior be removed. I get used to it and watch with a grain of salt or don't watch at all.. 18 Aug 2018 11:32

The Failing New York Times wrote a story that made it seem like the White House Councel had TURNED on the President when in fact it is just the opposite - & the two Fake reporters knew this. This is why the Fake News Media has become the Enemy of the People. So bad for America! 19 Aug 2018 12:06

Some members of the media are very Angry at the Fake Story in the New York Times. They actually called to complain and apologize - a big step forward. From the day I announced the Times has been Fake News and with their disgusting new Board Member it will only get worse! 19 Aug 2018 12:14

Fake News of which there is soooo much (this time the very tired New Yorker) falsely reported that I was going to take the extraordinary step of denying Intelligence Briefings to President Obama. Never discussed or thought of! 21 Aug 2018 11:10

Social Media Giants are silencing millions of people. Can't do this even if it means we must continue to hear Fake News like CNN whose ratings have suffered gravely. People have to figure out what is real and what is not without censorship! 24 Aug 2018 11:34

Michaels Cohen's attorney clarified the record saying his client does not know if President Trump knew about the Trump Tower meeting (out of which came nothing!). The answer is that I did NOT know about the meeting. Just another phony story by the Fake News Media! 25 Aug 2018 12:16

Over 90% approval rating for your all time favorite (I hope) President within the Republican Party and 52% overall. This despite all of the made up stories by the Fake News Media trying endlessly to make me look as bad and evil as possible. Look at the real villains please! 27 Aug 2018 0:39

The Fake News Media worked hard to get Tiger Woods to say something that he didn't want to say. Tiger wouldn't play the game - he is very smart. More importantly he is playing great golf again! 27 Aug 2018 13:37

Google search results for "Trump News" shows only the viewing/reporting of Fake News Media. In other words they have it RIGGED for me & others so that almost all stories & news is BAD. Fake CNN is prominent. Republican/Conservative & Fair Media is shut out. Illegal? 96% of.... 28 Aug 2018 15:02

"Anonymous Sources are really starting to BURN the media." @FoxNews The fact is that many anonymous sources don't even exist. They are fiction made up by the Fake News reporters. Look at the lie that Fake CNN is now in. They got caught red handed! Enemy of the People! 29 Aug 2018 12:40

CNN is being torn apart from within based on their being caught in a major lie and refusing to admit the mistake. Sloppy @carlbernstein a man who lives in the past and thinks like a degenerate fool making up story after story is being laughed at all over the country! Fake News 29 Aug 2018 22:43

"Lanny Davis admits being anonymous source in CNN Report." @BretBaier Oh well so much for CNN saying it wasn't Lanny. No wonder their ratings are so low it's FAKE NEWS! 30 Aug 2018 0:44

Ivanka Trump & Jared Kushner had NOTHING to do with the so called "pushing out" of Don McGahn.The Fake News Media has it purposelyso wrong! They love to portray chaos in the White House when they know that chaos doesn't exist-just a "smooth running machine" with changing parts! 30 Aug 2018 11:44

I am very excited about the person who will be taking the place of Don McGahn as White House Councel! I liked Don but he was NOT responsible for me not firing Bob Mueller or Jeff Sessions. So much Fake Reporting and Fake News! 30 Aug 2018 12:12

I am very excited about the person who will be taking the place of Don McGahn as White House Counsel! I liked Don but he was NOT responsible for me not firing Bob Mueller or Jeff Sessions. So much Fake Reporting and Fake News! 30 Aug 2018 13:39

.@Rasmussen_Poll just came out at 48% approval rate despite the constant and intense Fake News. Higher than Election Day and higher than President Obama. Rasmussen was one of the most accurate Election Day polls! 1 Sep 2018 2:25

RT @realDonaldTrump: .@Rasmussen_Poll just came out at 48% approval rate despite the constant and intense Fake News. Higher than Election D... 2 Sep 2018 14:10

NBC FAKE NEWS which is under intense scrutiny over their killing the Harvey Weinstein story is now fumbling around making excuses for their probably highly unethical conduct. I have long criticized NBC and their journalistic standards-worse than even CNN. Look at their license? 4 Sep 2018 14:58

The Deep State and the Left and their vehicle the Fake News Media are going Crazy - & they don't know what to do. The Economy is booming like never before Jobs are at Historic Highs soon TWO Supreme Court Justices & maybe Declassification to find Additional Corruption. Wow! 6 Sep 2018 11:19

When President Obama said that he has been to "57 States" very little mention in Fake News Media. Can you imagine if I said that...story of the year! @IngrahamAngle 15 Sep 2018 3:08

Watch @MariaBartiromo at 6:00 P.M. on @FoxBusiness. Russian Hoax the big topic! Mainstream Media often referred to as the Fake News Media hates to discuss the real facts! 16 Sep 2018 21:40

The crowd in front of the U.S. Supreme Court is tiny looks like about 200 people (& most are onlookers) - that wouldn't even fill the first couple of rows of our Kansas Rally or any of our Rallies for that matter! The Fake News Media tries to make it look sooo big & it's not! 6 Oct 2018 21:57

Despite so many positive events and victories Media Reseach Center reports that 92% of stories on Donald Trump are negative on ABC CBS and ABC. It is FAKE NEWS! Don't worry the Failing New York Times didn't even put the Brett Kavanaugh victory on the Front Page yesterday-A17! 10 Oct 2018 13:01

For the record I have no financial interests in Saudi Arabia (or Russia for that matter). Any suggestion that I have is just more FAKE NEWS (of which there is plenty)! 16 Oct 2018 13:15

AP headline was very different from my quote and meaning

in the story. They just can't help themselves. FAKE NEWS! 17 Oct 2018 12:09

Secretary of State Mike Pompeo was never given or shown a Transcript or Video of the Saudi Consulate event. FAKE NEWS! 19 Oct 2018 17:26

Facebook has just stated that they are setting up a system to "purge" themselves of Fake News. Does that mean CNN will finally be put out of business? 21 Oct 2018 22:48

The Fake News Media has been talking about recent approval ratings of me by countries around the world including the European Union as being very low.... 22 Oct 2018 19:18

A very big part of the Anger we see today in our society is caused by the purposely false and inaccurate reporting of the Mainstream Media that I refer to as Fake News. It has gotten so bad and hateful that it is beyond description. Mainstream Media must clean up its act FAST! 25 Oct 2018 11:18

The New York Times has a new Fake Story that now the Russians and Chinese (glad they finally added China) are listening to all of my calls on cellphones. Except that I rarely use a cellphone & when I do it's government authorized. I like Hard Lines. Just more made up Fake News! 25 Oct 2018 13:57

The Fake News is doing everything in their power to blame Republicans Conservatives and me for the division and hatred that has been going on for so long in our Country. Actually it is their Fake & Dishonest reporting which is causing problems far greater than they understand! 29 Oct 2018 0:12

There is great anger in our Country caused in part by inaccurate and even fraudulent reporting of the news. The Fake News Media the true Enemy of the People must stop the open & obvious hostility & report the news accurately & fairly. That will do much to put out the flame... 29 Oct 2018 12:03

....of Anger and Outrage and we will then be able to bring all sides together in Peace and Harmony. Fake News Must End! 29 Oct 2018 12:07

CNN and others in the Fake News Business keep purposely and inaccurately reporting that I said the "Media is the Enemy of the People." Wrong! I said that the "Fake News (Media) is the Enemy of the People" a very big difference. When you give out false information - not good! 30 Oct 2018 0:00

Check out tweets from last two days. I refer to Fake News Media when mentioning Enemy of the People - but dishonest reporters use only the word "Media." The people of our Great Country are angry and disillusioned at receiving so much Fake News. They get it and fully understand! 30 Oct 2018 0:14

Melania and I were treated very nicely yesterday in Pittsburgh. The Office of the President was shown great respect on a very sad and solemn day. We were treaty so warmly. Small protest was not seen by us staged far away. The Fake News stories were just the opposite-Disgraceful! 31 Oct 2018 13:01

Melania and I were treated very nicely yesterday in Pittsburgh. The Office of the President was shown great respect on a very sad & solemn day. We were treated so warmly. Small protest was not seen by us staged far away. The Fake News stories were just the opposite-Disgraceful! 31 Oct 2018 13:09

There is a rumor put out by the Democrats that Josh Hawley of Missouri left the Arena last night early. It is Fake News. He met me at the plane when I arrived spoke at the great Rally & stayed to the very end. In fact I said goodbye to him and left before he did. Deception! 6 Nov 2018 15:20

To any of the pundits or talking heads that do not give us proper credit for this great Midterm Election just remember two words - FAKE NEWS! 7 Nov 2018 12:52

By the way when the helicopter couldn't fly to the first cemetery in France because of almost zero visibility I suggested driving. Secret Service said NO too far from airport & big Paris shutdown. Speech next day at American Cemetary in pouring rain! Little reported-Fake News! 13 Nov 2018 13:30

By the way when the helicopter couldn't fly to the first cemetery in France because of almost zero visibility I suggested driving. Secret Service said NO too far from airport & big Paris shutdown. Speech next day at American Cemetery in pouring rain! Little reported-Fake News! 13 Nov 2018 15:49

The story in the New York Times concerning North Korea developing missile bases is inaccurate. We fully know about the sites being discussed nothing new - and nothing happening out of the normal. Just more Fake News. I will be the first to let you know if things go bad! 13 Nov 2018 17:07

The White House is running very smoothly and the results for our Nation are obviously very good. We are the envy of the world. But anytime I even think about making changes the FAKE NEWS MEDIA goes crazy always seeking to make us look as bad as possible! Very dishonest! 15 Nov 2018 11:59

People are not being told that the Republican Party is on track to pick up two seats in the U.S. Senate and epic victory: 53 to 47. The Fake News Media only wants to speak of the House were the Midterm results were better than other sitting Presidents. 16 Nov 2018 19:35

People are not being told that the Republican Party is on track to pick up two seats in the U.S. Senate and epic victory: 53 to 47. The Fake News Media only wants to speak of the House where the Midterm results were better than other sitting Presidents. 16 Nov 2018 19:41

....I can't imagine any President having a better or closer relationship with their Vice President then the two of us. Just more FAKE NEWS the Enemy of the People! 17 Nov 2018 16:42

The Fake News is showing old footage of people climbing over our Ocean Area Fence. This is what it really looks like - no climbers anymore under our Administration! 19 Nov 2018 19:10

You just can't win with the Fake News Media. A big story today is that because I have pushed so hard and gotten Gasoline Prices so low more people are driving and I have caused traffic jams throughout our Great Nation. Sorry everyone! 22 Nov 2018 0:36

I am extremely happy and proud of the job being done by @USTreasury Secretary @StevenMnuchin1. The FAKE NEWS likes to write stories to the contrary quoting phony sources or jealous people but they aren't true. They never like to ask me for a quote b/c it would kill their story. 23 Nov 2018 23:48

RT @realDonaldTrump: The Fake News is showing old footage of people climbing over our Ocean Area Fence. This is what it really looks like -... 23 Nov 2018 23:49

....The Fake News Media builds Bob Mueller up as a Saint when in actuality he is the exact opposite. He is doing TREMENDOUS damage to our Criminal Justice System where he is only looking at one side and not the other. Heroes will come of this and it won't be Mueller and his... 27 Nov 2018 12:42

While the disgusting Fake News is doing everything within their power not to report it that way at least 3 major players are intimating that the Angry Mueller Gang of Dems is viciously telling witnesses to lie about facts & they will get relief. This is our Joseph McCarthy Era! 28 Nov 2018 13:39

Does the Fake News Media ever mention the fact that Republicans with the very important help of my campaign Rallies WON THE UNITED STATES SENATE 53 to 47? All I hear is that the Open Border Dems won the House. Senate alone approves judges & others. Big Republican Win! 7 Dec 2018 0:27

FAKE NEWS - THE ENEMY OF THE PEOPLE! 7 Dec 2018 3:08

It has been incorrectly reported that Rudy Giuliani and others will not be doing a counter to the Mueller Report. That is Fake News. Already 87 pages done but obviously cannot complete until we see the final Witch Hunt Report. 7 Dec 2018 13:39

The Trump Administration has accomplished more than any other U.S. Administration in its first two (not even) years of existence & we are having a great time doing it! All of this despite the Fake News Media which has gone totally out of its mind-truly the Enemy of the People! 9 Dec 2018 22:43

I am in the process of interviewing some really great people for the position of White House Chief of Staff. Fake News has been saying with certainty it was Nick Ayers a spectacular person who will always be with our #MAGA agenda. I will be making a decision soon! 10 Dec 2018 1:27

Fake News has it purposely wrong. Many over ten are vying for and wanting the White House Chief of Staff position. Why wouldn't someone want one of the truly great and meaningful jobs in Washington. Please report news correctly. Thank you! 11 Dec 2018 13:30

Wow 19000 Texts between Lisa Page and her lover Peter S of the FBI in charge of the Russia Hoax were just reported as being wiped clean and gone. Such a big story that will never be covered by the Fake News. Witch Hunt! 15 Dec 2018 16:45

....Russia Iran Syria & many others are not happy about the U.S. leaving despite what the Fake News says because now they will have to fight ISIS and others who they hate without us. I am building by far the most powerful military in the world. ISIS hits us they are doomed! 20 Dec 2018 12:16

There has never been a president who has been tougher (but fair) on China or Russia - Never just look at the facts. The Fake News tries so hard to paint the opposite picture. 21 Dec 2018 14:41

Brett McGurk who I do not know was appointed by President Obama in 2015. Was supposed to leave in February but he just resigned prior to leaving. Grandstander? The Fake News is making such a big deal about this nothing event! 23 Dec 2018 1:48

If anybody but your favorite President Donald J. Trump announced that after decimating ISIS in Syria we were going to bring our troops back home (happy & healthy) that person would be the most popular hero in America. With me hit hard instead by the Fake News Media. Crazy! 23 Dec 2018 1:59

We signed two pieces of major legislation this week Criminal Justice Reform and the Farm Bill. These are two Big Deals but all the Fake News Media wants to talk about is "the mistake" of bringing our young people back home from the Never Ending Wars. It all began 19 years ago! 23 Dec 2018 19:45

I never "lashed out" at the Acting Attorney General of the U.S. a man for whom I have great respect. This is a made up story one of many by the Fake News Media! 24 Dec 2018 16:55

I hope everyone even the Fake News Media is having a great Christmas! Our Country is doing very well. We are securing our Borders making great new Trade Deals and bringing our Troops Back Home. We are finally putting America First. MERRY CHRISTMAS! #MAGA 25 Dec 2018 23:18

CNN & others within the Fake News Universe were going wild about my signing MAGA hats for our military in Iraq and Germany. If these brave young people ask me to sign their hat I will sign. Can you imagine my saying NO? We brought or gave NO hats as the Fake News first reported! 27 Dec 2018 23:23

...I campaigned on getting out of Syria and other places. Now when I start getting out the Fake News Media or some failed Generals who were unable to do the job before I arrived like to complain about me & my tactics which are working. Just doing what I said I was going to do! 31 Dec 2018 13:12

I am the only person in America who could say that "I'm

bringing our great troops back home with victory" and get BAD press. It is Fake News and Pundits who have FAILED for years that are doing the complaining. If I stayed in Endless Wars forever they would still be unhappy! 31 Dec 2018 14:38

Rocket Man

.@DennisRodman must be thinking of North Korea. #CelebApprentice 4 Mar 2013 2:31

How much is South Korea paying the U.S. for protection against North Korea???? NOTHING! 9 Mar 2013 10:36

North Korea is reliant on China. China could solve this problem easily if they wanted to but they have no respect for our leaders. 30 Mar 2013 11:33

What do we get from our economic competitor South Korea for the tremendous cost of protecting them from North Korea? - NOTHING! 30 Mar 2013 11:42

China has control over North Korea! 2 Apr 2013 19:48

I ask again how much is very wealthy South Korea paying the United States for protecting it against North Korea? 2 Apr 2013 20:48

North Korea can't survive or even eat without the help of China. China could solve this problem with one phone call-they love taunting us! 5 Apr 2013 13:08

Our President must be very careful with the 28 year old wack job in North Korea. At some point we may have to get very tough-blatant threats 6 Apr 2013 22:47

China is pushing North Korea! 6 Apr 2013 23:08

.@foxandfriends interview re: North Korea firing @dennisrodman job report @MELANIATRUMP's debut & @WrestleMania 8 Apr 2013 16:31

China controls North Korea. So now besides cyber hacking us all day they are using the Norks to taunt us. China is a major threat. 12 Apr 2013 19:26

The only American who has met with the North Korean man child is Dennis Rodman. Isn't that frightening and sad? 12 Apr 2013 19:47

Where is the President? It is time for him to come on TV and show strength against the repeated threats from North Korea -- and others. 12 Apr 2013 19:49

China will extract much from Secretary Kerry and the U:S. in order for them to help us with the North Korea problem-don't let this happen! 13 Apr 2013 23:24

Obama is now warning North Korea on the Yongbyon nuclear reactor. After Syria our enemies are laughing! 13 Sep 2013 20:24

Do you think John Kerry is aware of the fact that they are building nuclear weapons in Iran and North Korea and Pakistan already has them!! 18 Feb 2014 0:31

Crazy Dennis Rodman is saying I wanted to go to North Korea with him. Never discussed no interest last place on Earth I want to go to. 8 May 2014 1:34

Dennis Rodman was either drunk or on drugs (delusional) when he said I wanted to go to North Korea with him. Glad I fired him on Apprentice! 8 May 2014 1:39

CLINTON IS WEAK ON NORTH KOREA: #VPDebate 5 Oct 2016 2:19

North Korea just stated that it is in the final stages of developing a nuclear weapon capable of reaching parts of the U.S. It won't happen! 2 Jan 2017 23:05

China has been taking out massive amounts of money & wealth from the U.S. in totally one-sided trade but won't help with North Korea. Nice! 2 Jan 2017 23:47

#ICYMI: Joint Statement with Prime Minister Shinzo Abe on North Korea. 12 Feb 2017 5:02

North Korea is behaving very badly. They have been "playing" the United States for years. China has done little to help! 17 Mar 2017 13:07

I explained to the President of China that a trade deal with the U.S. will be far better for them if they solve the North Korean problem! 11 Apr 2017 11:59

North Korea is looking for trouble. If China decides to help that would be great. If not we will solve the problem without them! U.S.A. 11 Apr 2017 12:03

Had a very good call last night with the President of China concerning the menace of North Korea. 12 Apr 2017 12:22

I have great confidence that China will properly deal with North Korea. If they are unable to do so the U.S. with its allies will! U.S.A. 13 Apr 2017 13:08

Why would I call China a currency manipulator when they are working with us on the North Korean problem? We will see what happens! 16 Apr 2017 12:18

China is very much the economic lifeline to North Korea so while nothing is easy if they want to solve the North Korean problem they will 21 Apr 2017 13:04

North Korea disrespected the wishes of China & its highly respected President when it launched though unsuccessfully a missile today. Bad! 28 Apr 2017 23:26

North Korea has shown great disrespect for their neighbor China by shooting off yet another ballistic missile...but China is trying hard! 29 May 2017 12:18

The U.S. once again condemns the brutality of the North Korean regime as we mourn its latest victim. Video 20 Jun 2017 16:41

While I greatly appreciate the efforts of President Xi & China to help with North Korea it has not worked out. At least I know China tried! 20 Jun 2017 18:38

Just finished a very good meeting with the President of South Korea. Many subjects discussed including North Korea and new trade deal! 30 Jun 2017 1:44

The era of strategic patience with the North Korea regime has failed. That patience is over. We are working closely... 30 Jun 2017 20:55

North Korea has just launched another missile. Does this guy have anything better to do with his life? Hard to believe that South Korea..... 4 Jul 2017 2:19

....and Japan will put up with this much longer. Perhaps China will put a heavy move on North Korea and end this nonsense once and for all! 4 Jul 2017 2:24

Trade between China and North Korea grew almost 40% in the first quarter. So much for China working with us - but we had to give it a try! 5 Jul 2017 11:21

Leaving Hamburg for Washington D.C. and the WH. Just left China's President Xi where we had an excellent meeting on trade & North Korea. 8 Jul 2017 18:55

...they do NOTHING for us with North Korea just talk. We will no longer allow this to continue. China could easily solve this problem! 29 Jul 2017 23:35

The United Nations Security Council just voted 15-0 to sanction North Korea. China and Russia voted with us. Very big financial impact! 5 Aug 2017 22:44

United Nations Resolution is the single largest economic sanctions package ever on North Korea. Over one billion dollars in cost to N.K. 5 Aug 2017 23:14

Just completed call with President Moon of South Korea. Very happy and impressed with 15-0 United Nations vote on North Korea sanctions. 7 Aug 2017 1:22

RT @foxandfriends: U.S. spy satellites detect North Korea moving anti-ship cruise missiles to patrol boat 8 Aug 2017 10:41

After many years of failurecountries are coming together to finally address the dangers posed by North Korea. We must be tough & decisive! 8 Aug 2017 11:17

RT @foxandfriends: Trump vows U.S. 'power' will meet North Korean threat 9 Aug 2017 11:23

RT @foxandfriends: President Trump vows America will respond to North Korean threats with "fire & fury" in a warning to the rogue nation ht... 9 Aug 2017 11:26

RT @TheFive: "@POTUS being unpredictable is a big asset North Korea knew exactly what President Obama was going to do."- @jessebwatters 10 Aug 2017 1:18

RT @foxandfriends: FOX NEWS ALERT: North Korea responds to U.S. with Guam attack plan as Secretary Mattis warns Kim Jung Un "he is grossly... 10 Aug 2017 11:17

Military solutions are now fully in placelocked and loadedshould North Korea act unwisely. Hopefully Kim Jong Un will find another path! 11 Aug 2017 11:29

RT @FoxNews: .@AlanDersh: Trump Has 'More Credibility' Than Obama With North Korea 13 Aug 2017 22:01

RT @foxandfriends: Sec. Mattis: If North Korea fires missile at US it's 'game on' 15 Aug 2017 2:38

Kim Jong Un of North Korea made a very wise and well reasoned decision. The alternative would have been both catastrophic and unacceptable! 16 Aug 2017 11:39

The U.S. has been talking to North Korea and paying them extortion money for 25 years. Talking is not the answer! 30 Aug 2017 12:47

North Korea has conducted a major Nuclear Test. Their words and actions continue to be very hostile and dangerous to the United States..... 3 Sep 2017 11:30

..North Korea is a rogue nation which has become a great threat and embarrassment to China which is trying to help but with little success. 3 Sep 2017 11:39

South Korea is finding as I have told them that their talk of appeasement with North Korea will not work they only understand one thing! 3 Sep 2017 11:46

I will be meeting General Kelly General Mattis and other military leaders at the White House to discuss North Korea. Thank you. 3 Sep 2017 16:07

The United States is considering in addition to other options stopping all trade with any country doing business with North Korea. 3 Sep 2017 16:14

I spoke with President Moon of South Korea last night. Asked him how Rocket Man is doing. Long gas lines forming in North Korea. Too bad! 17 Sep 2017 11:53

RT @RealEagleBites: @realDonaldTrump It is the height of hypocrisy. Obama and Clinton in effect gave nuclear weapons to North Korea by thei... 20 Sep 2017 10:47

Today I announced a new Executive Order with re: to North Korea. We must all do our part to ensure the complete denuclearization of #NoKo. 21 Sep 2017 17:58

Kim Jong Un of North Korea who is obviously a madman who doesn't mind starving or killing his people will be tested like never before! 22 Sep 2017 10:28

Iran just test-fired a Ballistic Missile capable of reaching Israel.They are also working with North Korea.Not much of an agreement we have! 23 Sep 2017 21:59

Just heard Foreign Minister of North Korea speak at U.N. If he echoes thoughts of Little Rocket Man they won't be around much longer! 24 Sep 2017 3:08

Great interview on @foxandfriends with the parents of Otto Warmbier: 1994 - 2017. Otto was tortured beyond belief by North Korea. 26 Sep 2017 11:14

I told Rex Tillerson our wonderful Secretary of State that he is wasting his time trying to negotiate with Little Rocket Man... 1 Oct 2017 14:30

Being nice to Rocket Man hasn't worked in 25 years why would it work now? Clinton failed Bush failed and Obama failed. I won't fail. 1 Oct 2017 19:01

Presidents and their administrations have been talking to North Korea for 25 years agreements made and massive amounts of money paid...... 7 Oct 2017 19:40

Our country has been unsuccessfully dealing with North Korea for 25 years giving billions of dollars & getting nothing. Policy didn't work! 9 Oct 2017 10:50

The North Korean regime has pursued its nuclear & ballistic missile programs in defiance of every assurance agreement & commmitment it has made to the U.S. and its allies. It's broken all of those commitments... 8 Nov 2017 3:12

My meetings with President Xi Jinping were very productive on both trade and the subject of North Korea. He is a highly respected and powerful representative of his people. It was great being with him and Madame Peng Liyuan! 9 Nov 2017 23:44

Met with President Putin of Russia who was at #APEC meetings. Good discussions on Syria. Hope for his help to solve along with China the dangerous North Korea crisis. Progress being made. 12 Nov 2017 0:16

When will all the haters and fools out there realize that having a good relationship with Russia is a good thing not a bad thing. There always playing politics - bad for our country. I want to solve North Korea Syria Ukraine terrorism and Russia can greatly help! 12 Nov 2017 0:18

Why would Kim Jong-un insult me by calling me "old" when I would NEVER call him "short and fat?" Oh well I try so hard to be his friend - and maybe someday that will happen! 12 Nov 2017 0:48

China is sending an Envoy and Delegation to North Korea - A big move we'll see what happens! 16 Nov 2017 12:43

Just spoke to President XI JINPING of China concerning the provocative actions of North Korea. Additional major sanctions will be imposed on North Korea today. This situation will be handled! 29 Nov 2017 14:40

The Chinese Envoy who just returned from North Korea seems to have had no impact on Little Rocket Man. Hard to believe his people and the military put up with living in such horrible conditions. Russia and China condemned the launch. 30 Nov 2017 12:25

The United Nations Security Council just voted 15-0 in favor of additional Sanctions on North Korea. The World wants Peace not Death! 22 Dec 2017 20:47

Caught RED HANDED - very disappointed that China is allowing oil to go into North Korea. There will never be a friendly solution to the North Korea problem if this continues to happen! 28 Dec 2017 16:24

The Wall Street Journal stated falsely that I said to them "I have a good relationship with Kim Jong Un" (of N. Korea). Obviously I didn't say that. I said "I'd have a good relationship with Kim Jong Un" a big difference. Fortunately we now record conversations with reporters... 14 Jan 2018 12:58

I will be meeting with Henry Kissinger at 1:45pm. Will be discussing North Korea China and the Middle East. 8 Feb 2018 18:44

Possible progress being made in talks with North Korea. For the first time in many years a serious effort is being made by all parties concerned. The World is watching and waiting! May be false hope but the U.S. is ready to go hard in either direction! 6 Mar 2018 14:11

Kim Jong Un talked about denuclearization with the South Korean Representatives not just a freeze. Also no missile testing by North Korea during this period of time. Great progress being made but sanctions will remain until an agreement is reached. Meeting being planned! 9 Mar 2018 1:08

The deal with North Korea is very much in the making and will be if completed a very good one for the World. Time and place to be determined. 10 Mar 2018 0:42

Chinese President XI XINPING and I spoke at length about the meeting with KIM JONG UN of North Korea. President XI told me he appreciates that the U.S. is working to solve the problem diplomatically rather than going with the ominous alternative. China continues to be helpful! 10 Mar 2018 15:22

Chinese President XI JINPING and I spoke at length about the meeting with KIM JONG UN of North Korea. President XI told me he appreciates that the U.S. is working to solve the problem diplomatically rather than going with the ominous alternative. China continues to be helpful! 10 Mar 2018 16:15

Spoke to Prime Minister Abe of Japan who is very enthusiastic about talks with North Korea. Also discussing opening up Japan to much better trade with the U.S. Currently have a massive $100 Billion Trade Deficit. Not fair or sustainable. It will all work out! 10 Mar 2018 17:23

North Korea has not conducted a Missile Test since November 28 2017 and has promised not to do so through our meetings. I believe they will honor that commitment! 10 Mar 2018 18:38

In the first hours after hearing that North Korea's leader wanted to meet with me to talk denuclearization and that missile launches will end the press was startled & amazed. They couldn't believe it. But by the following morning the news became FAKE.They said so what who cares! 10 Mar 2018 20:02

.....They can help solve problems with North Korea Syria Ukraine ISIS Iran and even the coming Arms Race. Bush tried to get along but didn't have the "smarts." Obama and Clinton tried but didn't have the energy or chemistry (remember RESET). PEACE THROUGH STRENGTH! 21 Mar 2018 19:05

For years and through many administrations everyone said that peace and the denuclearization of the Korean Peninsula was not even a small possibility. Now there is a good chance that Kim Jong Un will do what is right for his people and for humanity. Look forward to our meeting! 28 Mar 2018 10:05

Received message last night from XI JINPING of China that his meeting with KIM JONG UN went very well and that KIM looks forward to his meeting with me. In the meantime and unfortunately maximum sanctions and pressure must be maintained at all cost! 28 Mar 2018 10:16

Mike Pompeo met with Kim Jong Un in North Korea last week. Meeting went very smoothly and a good relationship was formed. Details of Summit are being worked out now. Denuclearization will be a great thing for World but also for North Korea! 18 Apr 2018 10:42

Great meeting with Prime Minister Abe of Japan who has just left Florida. Talked in depth about North Korea Military and Trade. Good things will happen! 19 Apr 2018 14:45

North Korea has agreed to suspend all Nuclear Tests and close up a major test site. This is very good news for North Korea and the World - big progress! Look forward to our Summit. 20 Apr 2018 22:50

A message from Kim Jong Un: "North Korea will stop nuclear tests and launches of intercontinental ballistic missiles."Also will "Shut down a nuclear test site in the country's Northern Side to prove the vow to suspend nuclear tests." Progress being made for all! 21 Apr 2018 3:22

....We are a long way from conclusion on North Korea maybe things will work out and maybe they won't - only time will tell....But the work I am doing now should have been done a long time ago! 22 Apr 2018 13:02

Funny how all of the Pundits that couldn't come close to making a deal on North Korea are now all over the place telling me how to make a deal! 22 Apr 2018 18:43

Please do not forget the great help that my good friend President Xi of China has given to the United States particularly at the Border of North Korea. Without him it would have been a much longer tougher process! 27 Apr 2018 11:50

Just had a long and very good talk with President Moon of South Korea. Things are going very well time and location of meeting with North Korea is being set. Also spoke to Prime Minister Abe of Japan to inform him of the ongoing negotiations. 28 Apr 2018 13:45

Delegation heading to China to begin talks on the Massive Trade Deficit that has been created with our Country. Very much like North Korea this should have been fixed years ago not now. Same with other countries and NAFTA...but it will all get done. Great Potential for USA! 1 May 2018 11:00

There was no Collusion (it is a Hoax) and there is no Obstruction of Justice (that is a setup & trap). What there is is Negotiations going on with North Korea over Nuclear War Negotiations going on with China over Trade Deficits Negotiations on NAFTA and much more. Witch Hunt! 2 May 2018 11:45

"This isn't some game. You are screwing with the work of the president of the United States." John Dowd March 2018. With North Korea China the Middle East and so much more there is not much time to be thinking about this especially since there was no Russian "Collusion." 2 May 2018 22:40

As everybody is aware the past Administration has long been asking for three hostages to be released from a North Korean Labor camp but to no avail. Stay tuned! 3 May 2018 0:53

I will be speaking to my friend President Xi of China this morning at 8:30. The primary topics will be Trade where good things will happen and North Korea where relationships and trust are building. 8 May 2018 11:22

I am pleased to inform you that Secretary of State Mike Pompeo is in the air and on his way back from North Korea with the 3 wonderful gentlemen that everyone is looking so forward to meeting. They seem to be in good health. Also good meeting with Kim Jong Un. Date & Place set. 9 May 2018 12:30

The highly anticipated meeting between Kim Jong Un and myself will take place in Singapore on June 12th. We will both try to make it a very special moment for World Peace! 10 May 2018 14:37

North Korea has announced that they will dismantle Nuclear Test Site this month ahead of the big Summit Meeting on June 12th. Thank you a very smart and gracious gesture! 12 May 2018 21:08

China must continue to be strong & tight on the Border of North Korea until a deal is made. The word is that recently the Border has become much more porous and more has been filtering in. I want this to happen and North Korea to be

VERY successful but only after signing! 21 May 2018 11:40

Sadly I was forced to cancel the Summit Meeting in Singapore with Kim Jong Un. 24 May 2018 16:18

RT @FoxNews: WATCH: @POTUS on his decision to cancel the planned North Korea summit. 24 May 2018 16:18

I have decided to terminate the planned Summit in Singapore on June 12th. While many things can happen and a great opportunity lies ahead potentially I believe that this is a tremendous setback for North Korea and indeed a setback for the world... 24 May 2018 16:57

Democrats are so obviously rooting against us in our negotiations with North Korea. Just like they are coming to the defense of MS 13 thugs saying that they are individuals & must be nurtured or asking to end your big Tax Cuts & raise your taxes instead. Dems have lost touch! 25 May 2018 12:04

Very good news to receive the warm and productive statement from North Korea. We will soon see where it will lead hopefully to long and enduring prosperity and peace. Only time (and talent) will tell! 25 May 2018 12:14

We are having very productive talks with North Korea about reinstating the Summit which if it does happen will likely remain in Singapore on the same date June 12th. and if necessary will be extended beyond that date. 26 May 2018 0:37

Unlike what the Failing and Corrupt New York Times would like people to believe there is ZERO disagreement within the Trump Administration as to how to deal with North Korea... and if there was it wouldn't matter. The @nytimes has called me wrong right from the beginning! 26 May 2018 15:03

Our United States team has arrived in North Korea to make arrangements for the Summit between Kim Jong Un and myself. I truly believe North Korea has brilliant potential and will be a great economic and financial Nation one day. Kim Jong Un agrees with me on this. It will happen! 27 May 2018 20:09

We have put a great team together for our talks with North Korea. Meetings are currently taking place concerning Summit and more. Kim Young Chol the Vice Chairman of North Korea heading now to New York. Solid response to my letter thank you! 29 May 2018 10:30

Sorry I've got to start focusing my energy on North Korea Nuclear bad Trade Deals VA Choice the Economy rebuilding the Military and so much more and not on the Rigged Russia Witch Hunt that should be investigating Clinton/Russia/FBI/Justice/Obama/Comey/Lynch etc. 29 May 2018 11:27

Very good meetings with North Korea. 31 May 2018 13:15

Meeting in Singapore with North Korea will hopefully be the start of something big...we will soon see! 5 Jun 2018 11:34

Isn't it Ironic? Getting ready to go to the G-7 in Canada to fight for our country on Trade (we have the worst trade deals ever made) then off to Singapore to meet with North Korea & the Nuclear Problem...But back home we still have the 13 Angry Democrats pushing the Witch Hunt! 7 Jun 2018 11:57

Looking forward to seeing my friend Prime Minister @AbeShinzo of Japan at noon. Will be discussing North Korea and Trade. 7 Jun 2018 14:01

Obama Schumer and Pelosi did NOTHING about North Korea and now weak on Crime High Tax Schumer is telling me what to do at the Summit the Dems could never set up. Schumer failed with North Korea and Iran we don't need his advice! 8 Jun 2018 10:06

I am heading for Canada and the G-7 for talks that will mostly center on the long time unfair trade practiced against the United States. From there I go to Singapore and talks with North Korea on Denuclearization. Won't be talking about the Russian Witch Hunt Hoax for a while! 8 Jun 2018 11:22

I am on my way to Singapore where we have a chance to achieve a truly wonderful result for North Korea and the World. It will certainly be an exciting day and I know that Kim Jong-un will work very hard to do something that has rarely been done before... 9 Jun 2018 20:58

Heading back home from Singapore after a truly amazing visit. Great progress was made on the denuclearization of North Korea. Hostages are back home will be getting the remains of our great heroes back to their families no missiles shot no research happening sites closing... 12 Jun 2018 20:40

...Got along great with Kim Jong-un who wants to see wonderful things for his country. As I said earlier today: Anyone can make war but only the most courageous can make peace!

#SingaporeSummit 12 Jun 2018 20:40

Here is the video "A Story of Opportunity" that I shared with Kim Jong-un at the #SingaporeSummit 12 Jun 2018 21:23

I want to thank Chairman Kim for taking the first bold step toward a bright new future for his people. Our unprecedented meeting – the first between an American President and a leader of North Korea – proves that real change is possible! 13 Jun 2018 0:11

A year ago the pundits & talking heads people that couldn't do the job before were begging for conciliation and peace - "please meet don't go to war." Now that we meet and have a great relationship with Kim Jong Un the same haters shout out "you shouldn't meet do not meet!" 13 Jun 2018 1:14

Just landed - a long trip but everybody can now feel much safer than the day I took office. There is no longer a Nuclear Threat from North Korea. Meeting with Kim Jong Un was an interesting and very positive experience. North Korea has great potential for the future! 13 Jun 2018 9:56

Before taking office people were assuming that we were going to War with North Korea. President Obama said that North Korea was our biggest and most dangerous problem. No longer - sleep well tonight! 13 Jun 2018 10:01

The Republican Party is starting to show very big numbers. People are starting to see what is being done. Results are speaking loudly. North Korea and our greatest ever economy are leading the way! 14 Jun 2018 12:34

Now that I am back from Singapore where we had a great result with respect to North Korea the thought process must sadly go back to the Witch Hunt always remembering that there was No Collusion and No Obstruction of the fabricated No Crime. 14 Jun 2018 15:08

The denuclearization deal with North Korea is being praised and celebrated all over Asia. They are so happy! Over here in our country some people would rather see this historic deal fail than give Trump a win even if it does save potentially millions & millions of lives! 17 Jun 2018 13:01

RT @EricTrump: It is hard to believe that the historic North Korea / Kim Jong Un summit was exactly one week ago. Truly amazing to see the... 20 Jun 2018 13:43

I have confidence that Kim Jong Un will honor the contract we signed & even more importantly our handshake. We agreed to the denuclearization of North Korea. China on the other hand may be exerting negative pressure on a deal because of our posture on Chinese Trade-Hope Not! 9 Jul 2018 14:25

A very nice note from Chairman Kim of North Korea. Great progress being made! 12 Jul 2018 16:32

....Russia has agreed to help with North Korea where relationships with us are very good and the process is moving along. There is no rush the sanctions remain! Big benefits and exciting future for North Korea at end of process! 18 Jul 2018 10:16

....proliferation cyber attacks trade Ukraine Middle East peace North Korea and more. There are many answers some easy and some hard to these problems...but they can ALL be solved! 19 Jul 2018 13:30

The Remains of American Servicemen will soon be leaving North Korea and heading to the United States! After so many years this will be a great moment for so many families. Thank you to Kim Jong Un. 27 Jul 2018 3:50

Thank you to Chairman Kim Jong Un for keeping your word & starting the process of sending home the remains of our great and beloved missing fallen! I am not at all surprised that you took this kind action. Also thank you for your nice letter - I look forward to seeing you soon! 2 Aug 2018 4:47

Mark Levin "When they had power they didn't stop the Russians the Chinese the North Koreans they funded the Iranians & are responsible for the greatest scandal in American history by interfering with our election & trying to undermine the Trump Campaign and Trump Presidency." 16 Aug 2018 2:31

I have asked Secretary of State Mike Pompeo not to go to North Korea at this time because I feel we are not making sufficient progress with respect to the denuclearization of the Korean Peninsula... 24 Aug 2018 17:36

...Secretary Pompeo looks forward to going to North Korea in the near future most likely after our Trading relationship with China is resolved. In the meantime I would like to send my warmest regards and respect to Chairman Kim. I look forward to seeing him soon! 24 Aug 2018 17:36

STATEMENT FROM THE WHITE HOUSEPresident Donald J. Trump feels strongly that North Korea is under tremendous pressure from China because of our major trade disputes with the Chinese Government. At the same time we also know that China is providing North Korea with... 29 Aug 2018 21:23

...considerable aid including money fuel fertilizer and various other commodities. This is not helpful! Nonetheless the President believes that his relationship with Kim Jong Un is a very good and warm one and there is no reason at this time to be spending large amounts... 29 Aug 2018 21:23

Kim Jong Un of North Korea proclaims "unwavering faith in President Trump." Thank you to Chairman Kim. We will get it done together! 6 Sep 2018 10:58

North Korea has just staged their parade celebrating 70th anniversary of founding without the customary display of nuclear missiles. Theme was peace and economic development. "Experts believe that North Korea cut out the nuclear missiles to show President Trump...... 9 Sep 2018 15:21

...its commitment to denuclearize." @FoxNews This is a big and very positive statement from North Korea. Thank you To Chairman Kim. We will both prove everyone wrong! There is nothing like good dialogue from two people that like each other! Much better than before I took office. 9 Sep 2018 15:31

Kim Jong Un has agreed to allow Nuclear inspections subject to final negotiations and to permanently dismantle a test site and launch pad in the presence of international experts. In the meantime there will be no Rocket or Nuclear testing. Hero remains to continue being........ 19 Sep 2018 4:04

"North Korea recommits to denuclearization - we've come a long way." @FoxNews 19 Sep 2018 11:43

...North Korea to be identified as a result of my Summit with Chairman Kim. These HEROES are home they may Rest In Peace and hopefully their families can have closure. 20 Sep 2018 18:10

Just had a long and very good conversation with President Xi Jinping of China. We talked about many subjects with a heavy emphasis on Trade. Those discussions are moving along nicely with meetings being scheduled at the G-20 in Argentina.

Also had good discussion on North Korea! 1 Nov 2018 14:09

President Xi and I have a very strong and personal relationship. He and I are the only two people that can bring about massive and very positive change on trade and far beyond between our two great Nations. A solution for North Korea is a great thing for China and ALL! 3 Dec 2018 13:18

Many people have asked how we are doing in our negotiations with North Korea - I always reply by saying we are in no hurry there is wonderful potential for great economic success for that country.... 14 Dec 2018 18:17

....Kim Jong Un sees it better than anyone and will fully take advantage of it for his people. We are doing just fine! 14 Dec 2018 18:17

Christmas Eve briefing with my team working on North Korea – Progress being made. Looking forward to my next summit with Chairman Kim! 24 Dec 2018 21:14

Obstructionist Losers

@TheAme19: @realDonaldTrump @RedNationRising And the answer ISN'T Hillary or Pocahontas Warren for $300... 11 Aug 2014 8:58

@robertpizorno: I really want to hear @realDonaldTrump say You're fired to Reid and Pelosi. 7 Nov 2014 11:48

@elizabethforma Goofy Elizabeth Warren sometimes referred to as Pocahontas because she faked the fact she is native American is a lowlife! 25 May 2016 5:37

@elizabethforma Goofy Elizabeth Warren sometimes known as Pocahontas bought foreclosed housing and made a quick killing. Total hypocrite! 25 May 2016 12:17

I find it offensive that Goofy Elizabeth Warren sometimes referred to as Pocahontas pretended to be Native American to get in Harvard. 26 May 2016 21:15

Pocahontas is at it again! Goofy Elizabeth Warren one of the least productive U.S. Senators has a nasty mouth. Hope she is V.P. choice. 10 Jun 2016 12:07

Goofy Elizabeth Warren sometimes referred to as Pocahontas pretended to be a Native American in order to advance her career. Very racist! 11 Jun 2016 23:28

Pocahontas bombed last night! Sad to watch. 26 Jul 2016 12:42

I have always had a good relationship with Chuck Schumer. He is far smarter than Harry R and has the ability to get things done. Good news! 20 Nov 2016 14:05

like the 116% hike in Arizona. Also deductibles are so high that it is practically useless. Don't let the Schumer clowns out of this web... 4 Jan 2017 14:01

The Democrats lead by head clown Chuck Schumer know how bad ObamaCare is and what a mess they are in. Instead of working to fix it they.. 5 Jan 2017 11:57

protesters and the tears of Senator Schumer. Secretary Kelly said that all is going well with very few problems. MAKE AMERICA SAFE AGAIN! 30 Jan 2017 12:20

Nancy Pelosi and Fake Tears Chuck Schumer held a rally at the steps of The Supreme Court and mic did not work (a mess)-just like Dem party! 31 Jan 2017 11:21

We should start an immediate investigation into @SenSchumer and his ties to Russia and Putin. A total hypocrite! 3 Mar 2017 17:54

I hear by demand a second investigation after Schumer of Pelosi for her close ties to Russia and lying about it. 3 Mar 2017 20:47

I hearby demand a second investigation after Schumer of Pelosi for her close ties to Russia and lying about it. 3 Mar 2017 20:49

I hearby demand a second investigation after Schumer of Pelosi for her close ties to Russia and lying about it. 3 Mar 2017 20:49

I hereby demand a second investigation after Schumer of Pelosi for her close ties to Russia and lying about it. 3 Mar 2017 21:02

I hereby demand a second investigation after Schumer of Pelosi for her close ties to Russia and lying about it. 3 Mar 2017 21:02

Cryin' Chuck Schumer stated recently I do not have confidence in him (James Comey) any longer." Then acts so indignant. #draintheswamp 10 May 2017 2:42

Arizona had a 116% increase in ObamaCare premiums last year with deductibles very high. Chuck Schumer sold John McCain a bill of goods. Sad 23 Sep 2017 10:50

I called Chuck Schumer yesterday to see if the Dems want to do a great HealthCare Bill. ObamaCare is badly broken big premiums. Who knows! 7 Oct 2017 12:17

Dem Senator Schumer hated the Iran deal made by President Obama but now that I am involved he is OK with it. Tell that to Israel Chuck! 16 Oct 2017 12:49

The terrorist came into our country through what is called

the "Diversity Visa Lottery Program" a Chuck Schumer beauty. I want merit based. 1 Nov 2017 11:24

Senator Chuck Schumer helping to import Europes problems said Col.Tony Shaffer. We will stop this craziness! @foxandfriends 1 Nov 2017 11:40

The last thing we need in Alabama and the U.S. Senate is a Schumer/Pelosi puppet who is WEAK on Crime WEAK on the Border Bad for our Military and our great Vets Bad for our 2nd Amendment AND WANTS TO RAISES TAXES TO THE SKY. Jones would be a disaster! 26 Nov 2017 13:52

I endorsed Luther Strange in the Alabama Primary. He shot way up in the polls but it wasn't enough. Can't let Schumer/Pelosi win this race. Liberal Jones would be BAD! 26 Nov 2017 14:33

The jury was not told the killer of Kate was a 7 time felon. The Schumer/Pelosi Democrats are so weak on Crime that they will pay a big price in the 2018 and 2020 Elections. 1 Dec 2017 11:13

Putting Pelosi/Schumer Liberal Puppet Jones into office in Alabama would hurt our great Republican Agenda of low on taxes tough on crime strong on military and borders...& so much more. Look at your 401-k's since Election. Highest Stock Market EVER! Jobs are roaring back! 4 Dec 2017 12:00

LAST thing the Make America Great Again Agenda needs is a Liberal Democrat in Senate where we have so little margin for victory already. The Pelosi/Schumer Puppet Jones would vote against us 100% of the time. He's bad on Crime Life Border Vets Guns & Military. VOTE ROY MOORE! 8 Dec 2017 15:06

A big contingent of very enthusiastic Roy Moore fans at the rally last night. We can't have a Pelosi/Schumer Liberal Democrat Jones in that important Alabama Senate seat. Need your vote to Make America Great Again! Jones will always vote against what we must do for our Country. 9 Dec 2017 12:52

Lightweight Senator Kirsten Gillibrand a total flunky for Chuck Schumer and someone who would come to my office "begging" for campaign contributions not so long ago (and would do anything for them) is now in the ring fighting against Trump. Very disloyal to Bill & Crooked-USED! 12 Dec 2017 13:03

Excellent preliminary meeting in Oval with @SenSchumer - working on solutions for Security and our great Military together with @SenateMajLdr McConnell and @SpeakerRyan. Making progress - four week extension would be best! 19 Jan 2018 22:17

DACA has been made increasingly difficult by the fact that Cryin' Chuck Schumer took such a beating over the shutdown that he is unable to act on immigration! 26 Jan 2018 17:16

March 5th is rapidly approaching and the Democrats are doing nothing about DACA. They Resist Blame Complain and Obstruct - and do nothing. Start pushing Nancy Pelosi and the Dems to work out a DACA fix NOW! 1 Feb 2018 11:51

The Democrats just aren't calling about DACA. Nancy Pelosi and Chuck Schumer have to get moving fast or they'll disappoint you again. We have a great chance to make a deal or blame the Dems! March 5th is coming up fast. 2 Feb 2018 3:32

Rep. Lou Barletta a Great Republican from Pennsylvania who was one of my very earliest supporters will make a FANTASTIC Senator. He is strong & smart loves Pennsylvania & loves our Country! Voted for Tax Cuts unlike Bob Casey who listened to Tax Hikers Pelosi and Schumer! 11 Feb 2018 20:26

RT @SpoxDHS: Schumer-Rounds-Collins destroys the ability of @DHSgov to enforce immigration laws creating a mass amnesty for over 10 millio... 15 Feb 2018 19:22

Dems are no longer talking DACA! "Out of sight out of mind" they say. DACA beneficiaries should not be happy. Nancy Pelosi truly doesn't care about them. Republicans stand ready to make a deal! 24 Feb 2018 21:18

The Pittsburgh Post Gazette just endorsed Rick Saccone for Congress. He will be much better for steel and business. Very strong on experience and what our Country needs. Lamb will always vote for Pelosi and Dems....Will raise taxes weak on Crime and Border. 12 Mar 2018 14:43

Nancy Pelosi is going absolutely crazy about the big Tax Cuts given to the American People by the Republicans...got not one Democrat Vote! Here's a choice. They want to end them and raise your taxes substantially. Republicans are working on making them permanent and more cuts! 20 Apr 2018 10:50

The Republican Party had a great night. Tremendous voter energy and excitement and all candidates are those who have a great chance of winning in November. The Economy is sooo strong and with Nancy Pelosi wanting to end the big Tax Cuts and Raise Taxes why wouldn't we win? 9 May 2018 11:24

Senator Cryin' Chuck Schumer fought hard against the Bad Iran Deal even going at it with President Obama & then Voted AGAINST it! Now he says I should not have terminated the deal - but he doesn't really believe that! Same with Comey. Thought he was terrible until I fired him! 10 May 2018 14:30

Lou Barletta will be a great Senator for Pennsylvania but his opponent Bob Casey has been a do-nothing Senator who only shows up at election time. He votes along the Nancy Pelosi Elizabeth Warren lines loves sanctuary cities bad and expensive healthcare... 16 May 2018 18:40

I ask Senator Chuck Schumer why didn't President Obama & the Democrats do something about Trade with China including Theft of Intellectual Property etc.? They did NOTHING! With that being said Chuck & I have long agreed on this issue! Fair Trade plus with China will happen! 21 May 2018 11:21

Senator Schumer and Obama Administration let phone company ZTE flourish with no security checks. I closed it down then let it reopen with high level security guarantees change of management and board must purchase U.S. parts and pay a $1.3 Billion fine. Dems do nothing.... 25 May 2018 23:07

A Democratic lawmaker just introduced a bill to Repeal the GOP Tax Cuts (no chance). This is too good to be true for Republicans...Remember the Nancy Pelosi Dems are also weak on Crime the Border and want to be gentle and kind to MS-13 gang members...not good! 28 May 2018 21:22

Very importantly @RepDanDonovan will win for the Republicans in November...and his opponent will not. Remember Alabama. We can't take any chances on losing to a Nancy Pelosi controlled Democrat! 31 May 2018 0:08

Get the vote out in California today for Rep. Kevin McCarthy and all of the great GOP candidates for Congress. Keep our country out of the hands of High Tax High Crime Nancy Pelosi. 5 Jun 2018 13:09

Chuck Schumer said "the Summit was what the Texans call all cattle and no hat." Thank you Chuck but are you sure you got that right? No more nuclear testing or rockets flying all over the place blew up launch sites. Hostages already back hero remains coming home & much more! 17 Jun 2018 11:52

The Border has been a big mess and problem for many years. At some point Schumer and Pelosi who are weak on Crime and Border security will be forced to do a real deal so easy that solves this long time problem. Schumer used to want Border security - now he'll take Crime! 21 Jun 2018 12:29

Democrats want open Borders where anyone can come into our Country and stay. This is Nancy Pelosi's dream. It won't happen! 21 Jun 2018 14:38

Congresswoman Martha Roby of Alabama has been a consistent and reliable vote for our Make America Great Again Agenda. She is in a Republican Primary run-off against a recent Nancy Pelosi voting Democrat. I fully endorse Martha for Alabama 2nd Congressional District! 22 Jun 2018 11:46

...everyone how much he likes me but he will only vote with Nancy Pelosi. Keith is strong on borders and tough on crime — and loves cutting taxes! #MAGA 23 Jun 2018 14:00

It's very sad that Nancy Pelosi and her sidekick Cryin' Chuck Schumer want to protect illegal immigrants far more than the citizens of our country. The United States cannot stand for this. We wants safety and security at our borders! 23 Jun 2018 17:05

Congresswoman Maxine Waters an extraordinarily low IQ person has become together with Nancy Pelosi the Face of the Democrat Party. She has just called for harm to supporters of which there are many of the Make America Great Again movement. Be careful what you wish for Max! 25 Jun 2018 17:11

Wow! Big Trump Hater Congressman Joe Crowley who many expected was going to take Nancy Pelosi's place just LOST his primary election. In other words he's out! That is a big one that nobody saw happening. Perhaps he should have been nicer and more respectful to his President! 27 Jun 2018 2:18

Congratulations to Maxine Waters whose crazy rants have made her together with Nancy Pelosi the unhinged FACE of the Democrat Party. Together they will Make America Weak Again! But have no fear America is now stronger than ever before and I'm not going anywhere! 27 Jun 2018 11:18

Crazy Maxine Waters said by some to be one of the most corrupt people in politics is rapidly becoming together with Nancy Pelosi the FACE of the Democrat Party. Her ranting and raving even referring to herself as a wounded animal will make people flee the Democrats! 3 Jul 2018 10:16

Troy Balderson of Ohio is running for Congress against a Nancy Pelosi Liberal who is WEAK on Crime & Borders. Troy is the total opposite and loves our Military Vets & 2nd Amendment. EARLY VOTING just started with Election Day on August 7th. Troy has my Full & Total Endorsement! 21 Jul 2018 23:23

The only things the Democrats do well is "Resist" which is their campaign slogan and "Obstruct." Cryin' Chuck Schumer has almost 400 great American people that are waiting "forever" to serve our Country! A total disgrace. Mitch M should not let them go home until all approved! 28 Jul 2018 0:47

Will be going to Ohio tonight to campaign for Troy Balderson for the big Congressional Special Election on Tuesday. Early voting is on. Troy is strong on Crime the Border & loves our Military Vets & 2nd Amendment. His opponent is a puppet of Nancy Pelosi/high taxes. 4 Aug 2018 12:49

Troy Balderson running for Congress from Ohio is in a big Election fight with a candidate who just got caught lying about his relationship with Nancy Pelosi who is weak on Crime Borders & your 2nd Amendment-and wants to raise your Taxes (by a lot). Vote for Troy on Tuesday! 4 Aug 2018 13:02

...Danny O'Connor is a total puppet for Nancy Pelosi and Maxine Waters — Danny wants to raise your taxes open your borders and take away your 2nd Amendment. Vote for Troy on Tuesday! 5 Aug 2018 1:43

RT @realDonaldTrump: ...Danny O'Connor is a total puppet for Nancy Pelosi and Maxine Waters — Danny wants to raise your taxes open your bo... 5 Aug 2018 21:53

Ohio vote today for Troy Balderson for Congress. His opponent controlled by Nancy Pelosi is weak on Crime the Border Military Vets your 2nd Amendment - and will end your Tax Cuts. Troy will be a great Congressman. #MAGA 7 Aug 2018 10:46

Democrats please do not distance yourselves from Nancy Pelosi. She is a wonderful person whose ideas & policies may be bad but who should definitely be given a 4th chance. She is trying very hard & has every right to take down the Democrat Party if she has veered too far left! 10 Aug 2018 21:30

"People who enter the United States without our permission are illegal aliens and illegal aliens should not be treated the same as people who enters the U.S. legally." Chuck Schumer in 2009 before he went left and haywire! @foxandfriends 15 Aug 2018 12:44

"People who enter the United States without our permission are illegal aliens and illegal aliens should not be treated the same as people who entered the U.S. legally." Chuck Schumer in 2009 before he went left and haywire! @foxandfriends 15 Aug 2018 13:18

Happy Birthday to the leader of the Democrat Party Maxine Waters! 15 Aug 2018 14:57

Chuck Schumer I agree! 15 Aug 2018 18:34

Dave Hughes is running for Congress in the Great State of Minnesota. He will help us accomplish our America First policies is strong on Crime the Border our 2nd Amendmen Trade Military and Vets. Running against Pelosi Liberal Puppet Petterson. Dave has my Total Endorsement! 8 Sep 2018 14:44

Chuck Schumer is holding up 320 appointments (Ambassadors Executives etc.) of great people who have left jobs and given up so much in order to come into Government. Schumer and the Democrats continue to OBSTRUCT! 10 Sep 2018 21:18

Crazy Maxine Waters: "After we impeach Trump we'll go after Mike Pence. We'll get him." @FoxNews Where are the Democrats coming from? The best Economy in the history of our country would totally collapse if they ever took control! 12 Sep 2018 1:55

Congressman Bishop is doing a GREAT job! He helped pass tax reform which lowered taxes for EVERYONE! Nancy Pelosi is spending hundreds of thousands of dollars on his opponent because they both support a liberal agenda of higher taxes and wasteful spending! 4 Oct 2018 22:17

Highly respected Congressman Keith Rothfus (R) of Pennsylvania is in the fight of his life because the Dems changed the District Map. He must win. Strong on crime borders big tax & reg cuts Military & Vets. Opponent Lamb a Pelosi puppet-weak on crime. BIG ENDORSEMENT FOR KEITH 13 Oct 2018 17:43

Heading to the Great State of Kentucky - Big Rally for Congressman Andy Barr - Fantastic guy need his vote for MAGA! Strong on Crime Tax Cuts Military Vets & 2nd A. His opponent will NEVER vote for us only for Pelosi. Andy has my Strongest Endorsement!!! See you in Kentucky. 13 Oct 2018 17:52

Pocahontas (the bad version) sometimes referred to as Elizabeth Warren is getting slammed. She took a bogus DNA test and it showed that she may be 1/1024 far less than the average American. Now Cherokee Nation denies her "DNA test is useless." Even they don't want her. Phony! 16 Oct 2018 12:06

Thank you to the Cherokee Nation for revealing that Elizabeth Warren sometimes referred to as Pocahontas is a complete and total Fraud! 16 Oct 2018 12:24

Will be landing soon. Looking forward to seeing our next Senator from Montana Matt Rosendale. He will represent our Country well far better than Jon Tester who will vote with Cryin' Chuck Schumer and Nancy Pelosi - never with us! 19 Oct 2018 0:04

Jon Tester says one thing to voters and does the EXACT OPPOSITE in Washington. Tester takes his orders form Pelosi & Schumer. Tester wants to raise your taxes take away your 2A open your borders and deliver MOB RULE. Retire Tester & Elect America-First Patriot Matt Rosendale! 19 Oct 2018 3:11

Leaving Arizona after a fantastic Rally last night in Mesa honoring and for Martha @RepMcSally McSally. She is an inspiration & will be a GREAT SENATOR for the people of Arizona. Her opponent is a Nancy Pelosi puppet really bad for State. Early Voting NOW! Will be back soon. 20 Oct 2018 16:19

.@BrucePoliquin from Maine is a great Congressman. He is in a tough fight against a very liberal Nancy Pelosi Democrat. Bruce has helped bring JOBS back to his State and totally protects your Great Second Amendment. We need to keep Bruce in Washington. He has my Full Endorsement! 25 Oct 2018 20:39

Martha McSally is a great warrior her opponent a Nancy Pelosi Wacko! 27 Oct 2018 13:51

Congressman Andy Barr of Kentucky who just had a great debate with his Nancy Pelosi run opponent has been a winner for his State. Strong on Crime the Border Tax Cuts Military Vets and 2nd Amendment we need Andy in D.C. He has my Strong Endorsement! 30 Oct 2018 12:12

....Richard Cordray will let you down just like he did when he destroyed the government agency that he ran. Clone of Pocahontas that's not for Ohio. Mike has my Total Endorsement! 30 Oct 2018 17:37

I need the people of West Virginia to send a message to Chuck Schumer Maxine Waters Nancy Pelosi and the Radical Democrats by voting for Carol Miller and Patrick Morrisey! 2 Nov 2018 23:18

Congresswoman Maxine Waters was called the most Corrupt Member of Congress! @FoxNews If Dems win she would be put in charge of our Country's finances. The beginning of the end! 3 Nov 2018 10:54

If Chuck Schumer and Nancy Pelosi gain the majority they will try to raise your taxes restore job-killing regulations shut down your coal mines and timber mills take away your healthcare impose socialism and ERASE your borders. VOTE for @MattForMontana and @GregForMontana! 3 Nov 2018 20:38

If Chuck Schumer and Nancy Pelosi gain the majority they will try to raise your taxes restore job-killing regulations shut down your coal mines and timber mills take away your healthcare impose socialism and ERASE your borders. VOTE for @MattForMontana and @GregForMontana! 3 Nov 2018 20:38

RT @realDonaldTrump: I need the people of West Virginia to send a message to Chuck Schumer Maxine Waters Nancy Pelosi and the Radical Dem... 4 Nov 2018 15:25

RT @realDonaldTrump: Martha McSally is a great warrior her opponent a Nancy Pelosi Wacko! 4 Nov 2018 15:44

John James running as a Republican for the Senate from Michigan is a spectacular young star of the future. We should make him a star of the present. A distinguished West Point Grad and Vet people should Vote Out Schumer Puppet Debbie Stabenow who does nothing for Michigan! 5 Nov 2018 5:04

A vote for Claire McCaskill is a vote for Schumer Pelosi Waters and their socialist agenda. Claire voted IN FAVOR of deadly Sanctuary Cities - she would rather protect criminal aliens than American citizens which is why she needs to be voted out of office. Vote @HawleyMO! 6 Nov 2018 5:12

A vote for Claire McCaskill is a vote for Schumer Pelosi Waters and their socialist agenda. Claire voted IN FAVOR of deadly Sanctuary Cities - she would rather protect criminal aliens than American citizens which is why she needs to be voted out of office. Vote @HawleyMO! 6 Nov 2018 5:12

RT @realDonaldTrump: If Chuck Schumer and Nancy Pelosi gain the majority they will try to raise your taxes restore job-killing regulation... 6 Nov 2018 16:25

In all fairness Nancy Pelosi deserves to be chosen Speaker of the House by the Democrats. If they give her a hard time perhaps we will add some Republican votes. She has earned this great honor! 7 Nov 2018 13:31

I can get Nancy Pelosi as many votes as she wants in order for her to be Speaker of the House. She deserves this victory she has earned it - but there are those in her party who are trying to take it away. She will win! @TomReedCongress 17 Nov 2018 11:37

Really good Criminal Justice Reform has a true shot at major bipartisan support. @senatemajldr Mitch McConnell and @senchuckschumer have a real chance to do something so badly needed in our country. Already past with big vote in House. Would be a major victory for ALL! 23 Nov 2018 12:57

Really good Criminal Justice Reform has a true shot at major bipartisan support. @senatemajldr Mitch McConnell and @SenSchumer have a real chance to do something so badly needed in our country. Already passed with big vote in House. Would be a major victory for ALL! 23 Nov 2018 17:14

Soon to be Speaker Nancy Pelosi said last week live from the Oval Office that the Republicans didn't have the votes for Border Security. Today the House Republicans voted and won 217-185. Nancy does not have to apologize. All I want is GREAT BORDER SECURITY! 21 Dec 2018 3:20

Heads of countries are calling wanting to know why Senator Schumer is not approving their otherwise approved Ambassadors!? Likewise in Government lawyers and others are being delayed at a record pace! 360 great and hardworking people are waiting for approval from.... 31 Dec 2018 20:02

....Senator Schumer more than a year longer than any other Administration in history. These are people who have been approved by committees and all others yet Schumer continues to hold them back from serving their Country! Very Unfair! 31 Dec 2018 20:02

Great work by my Administration over the holidays to save Coast Guard pay during this #SchumerShutdown. No thanks to the Democrats who left town and are not concerned about the safety and security of Americans! 30 Dec 2018 16:56

Made in the USA
Middletown, DE
23 November 2020

24871611R00113